JavaScript and JSON Essentials

Successfully build advanced JSON-fueled web applications with this practical, hands-on guide

Sai Srinivas Sriparasa

 open source*
community experience distilled

PACKT PUBLISHING

BIRMINGHAM - MUMBAI

JavaScript and JSON Essentials

First published: October 2013

Production Reference: 1181013

Published by Packt Publishing Ltd.
Livery Place
35 Livery Street
Birmingham B3 2PB, UK.

ISBN 978-1-78328-603-4

www.packtpub.com

Cover image by Ravaji Babu (ravaji_babu@outlook.com)

Credits

Author
Sai Srinivas Sriparasa

Reviewers
Marco Lüthy
Shameera Rathnayaka

Acquisition Editor
Joanne Fitzpatrick

Lead Technical Editor
Shaon Basu

Technical Editors
Pooja Nair
Anusri Ramchandran
Amit Shetty
Ritika Singh

Copy Editors
Alisha Aranha
Brandt D'Mello
Lavina Pereira

Project Coordinator
Akash Poojary

Proofreader
Ting Baker

Indexer
Monica Ajmera Mehta

Production Coordinator
Kirtee Shingan

Cover Work
Kirtee Shingan

About the Author

Sai Srinivas Sriparasa is a web developer and an open source evangelist living in the Stamford area. Sai was the lead developer for building Dr. Oz's website, and has led teams for companies such as Sprint Nextel, West Interactive, and Apple. Sai's repertoire includes JavaScript, PHP, Python, HTML5, responsive web development, ASP.NET, C#, and Silverlight.

I want to convey my sincere thanks to the team at Packt Publishing for making this book possible, Shaon, Akash, and Sumeet in particular. This is my first book, so I want to thank all of the readers in advance for having taken the time to read my book. Please contact me on my LinkedIn profile `http://www.linkedin.com/in/saisriparasa` for networking or for any questions that you have.

My acknowledgments cannot be complete unless I thank my mom, dad, and sister for all their patience and support throughout my life. I hope you all enjoy this book and wish me luck for my next book.

About the Reviewers

Marco Lüthy is a Swiss-born creator, designer, developer, and engineer for Internet-enabled applications and has over 10 years of experience working on projects deployed over the Internet. Occasionally he likes to dabble in content creation of the written and photographic kind. Marco's current focus is the Tokyo-based Internet media and application development firm Robotag Media, Inc., where he is co-founder and resident factotum working on making many useful, pretty things for us all to use and play with.

Shameera Rathnayaka is an Apache Axis2 committer and a PMC member, and has been actively contributing to several Apache projects for the past few years. He holds a B.Sc. Engineering (Hons) in Computer Science and Engineering from the University of Moratuwa, Sri Lanka. He first started his open source contributions with the Apache Axis2 project, where he implemented JDK 7 Enum support for Apache Axis2 as well as stream-based high performance solutions for JSON<-->XML lossless transformation. He is a Google Summer of Code participant with Apache Axis2 and Apache Airavata projects and has reviewed the book *Instant GSON, Sandeep Kumar Patel, Packt Publishing*.

Shameera currently works as a Software Engineer at WSO2 Inc., an open source enterprise middleware company based in Sri Lanka, where he is a member of the WSO2 Carbon team. His main research interests are in distributed computing.

www.PacktPub.com

Support files, eBooks, discount offers and more

You might want to visit www.PacktPub.com for support files and downloads related to your book.

Did you know that Packt offers eBook versions of every book published, with PDF and ePub files available? You can upgrade to the eBook version at www.PacktPub.com and as a print book customer, you are entitled to a discount on the eBook copy. Get in touch with us at service@packtpub.com for more details.

At www.PacktPub.com, you can also read a collection of free technical articles, sign up for a range of free newsletters and receive exclusive discounts and offers on Packt books and eBooks.

http://PacktLib.PacktPub.com

Do you need instant solutions to your IT questions? PacktLib is Packt's online digital book library. Here, you can access, read and search across Packt's entire library of books.

Why Subscribe?

- Fully searchable across every book published by Packt
- Copy and paste, print and bookmark content
- On demand and accessible via web browser

Free Access for Packt account holders

If you have an account with Packt at www.PacktPub.com, you can use this to access PacktLib today and view nine entirely free books. Simply use your login credentials for immediate access.

Table of Contents

Preface

JavaScript and JSON Essentials is a one-stop resource that can be used for understanding and implementing JSON in various web applications. This book provides a comprehensive insight into how JSON can be implemented and integrated into your applications. Though JSON is one of the most popular data-exchange formats, the number of books available describing JSON and helping readers build a live solution is not high. This book is a comprehensive guide to JSON that begins with JavaScript basics, discusses the history of JSON, and then takes a step-by-step approach towards using JSON to build a live web application that is powered by JSON data.

What this book covers

Chapter 1, JavaScript Basics, is a basic refresher for common JavaScript concepts.

Chapter 2, Getting Started with JSON, introduces the audience to JSON, discusses the history of JSON, outlines the popular programming languages that support JSON, fires a Hello World program in JSON, and writes basic programs with different data types in JSON.

Chapter 3, Working with Real-time JSON, introduces the audience to complex JSON. The JSON used in this chapter will consist of multiple datatypes and multiple objects and will be multidimensional.

Chapter 4, AJAX Calls with JSON Data, goes over the requirements to successfully pass JSON over HTTP as JSON data has to transported over HTTP in real-world scenarios.

Chapter 5, Cross-domain Asynchronous Requests, introduces the audience to the concept of making asynchronous calls across domains. Since data is being transported across domains, users will be introduced to the concept of JSON with Padding.

Chapter 6, Building the Carousel Application, discusses the idea of a Carousel application and the required setup and dependencies such as, jQuery library, and jQuery Cycle plugin for the application.

Chapter 7, Alternate Implementations of JSON, discusses the non web-development implementation of JSON such as dependency managers, metadata stores, and configuration stores. The discussion would go forward and talk about the advantages of JSON over XML and YAML.

Chapter 8, Debugging JSON, introduces the powerful tools that are available to debug, validate, and format JSON. As the number of objects increases, the length of JSON increases too, which makes it difficult for the naked eye to validate JSON.

What you need for this book

JSON is language-and platform-independent, so readers can use an operating system of their choice. To serve live JSON, we need a live web server. There are parsers available for most of the popular server-side languages; readers can use a web server such as Apache, Tomcat, IIS, or any other web server and can pick a text editor of their choice.

Who this book is for

This book has been designed to cater to the needs of developers at all levels. This book contains numerous working examples, tips, and notes that will guide users through all the chapters. It is not required but would be good to have some knowledge about HTML and JavaScript. Some familiarity with server-side languages such as PHP, C#, or Python would be preferred, but not required.

Conventions

In this book, you will find a number of styles of text that distinguish between different kinds of information. Here are some examples of these styles, and an explanation of their meaning.

Code and the output being generated by the code are added to the book as screenshots. The name of the file will be shown as follows:.

```
json_helloworld.html
```

New terms and **important words** are shown in bold. Words that you see on the screen, in menus or dialog boxes for example, appear in the text like this: "Load the file in a web browser, and a pop-up box with the text **Hello World!** should be loaded on the page".

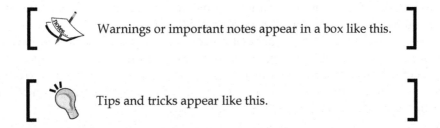

> Warnings or important notes appear in a box like this.

> Tips and tricks appear like this.

Reader feedback

Feedback from our readers is always welcome. Let us know what you think about this book — what you liked or may have disliked. Reader feedback is important for us to develop titles that you really get the most out of.

To send us general feedback, simply send an e-mail to feedback@packtpub.com, and mention the book title via the subject of your message.

If there is a topic that you have expertise in and you are interested in either writing or contributing to a book, see our author guide on www.packtpub.com/authors.

Customer support

Now that you are the proud owner of a Packt book, we have a number of things to help you to get the most from your purchase.

Downloading the example code

You can download the example code files for all Packt books you have purchased from your account at http://www.packtpub.com. If you purchased this book elsewhere, you can visit http://www.packtpub.com/support and register to have the files e-mailed directly to you.

Errata

Although we have taken every care to ensure the accuracy of our content, mistakes do happen. If you find a mistake in one of our books—maybe a mistake in the text or the code—we would be grateful if you would report this to us. By doing so, you can save other readers from frustration and help us improve subsequent versions of this book. If you find any errata, please report them by visiting http://www.packtpub.com/submit-errata, selecting your book, clicking on the **errata submission form** link, and entering the details of your errata. Once your errata are verified, your submission will be accepted and the errata will be uploaded on our website, or added to any list of existing errata, under the Errata section of that title. Any existing errata can be viewed by selecting your title from http://www.packtpub.com/support.

Piracy

Piracy of copyright material on the Internet is an ongoing problem across all media. At Packt, we take the protection of our copyright and licenses very seriously. If you come across any illegal copies of our works, in any form, on the Internet, please provide us with the location address or website name immediately so that we can pursue a remedy.

Please contact us at copyright@packtpub.com with a link to the suspected pirated material.

We appreciate your help in protecting our authors, and our ability to bring you valuable content.

Questions

You can contact us at questions@packtpub.com if you are having a problem with any aspect of the book, and we will do our best to address it.

1
JavaScript Basics

JavaScript, which was introduced as LiveScript by Netscape Communications Corp, has grown leaps and bounds in the last few years. JavaScript was originally developed to make web pages more interactive, and control the behavior of the page. JavaScript programs are commonly embedded inside an HTML file. HTML is a markup language, and does not manipulate the behavior of a page once its loaded. Using JavaScript, web developers can set rules and verify if the rules were followed, avoiding any remote server resources for input validation or complex number crunching. Today JavaScript is not just used for basic input validation; it is used to access the browser's `Document` object, to make asynchronous calls to the web server, and to develop end-to-end web applications using software platforms such as `Node.JS`, which is powered by Google's v8 JavaScript engine.

JavaScript is considered to be one of the three building blocks that are required to create interactive web pages; it is the only programming language in the trinity that is HTML, CSS, and JavaScript. JavaScript is a case sensitive and a space insensitive language, unlike Python and Ruby. A JavaScript program is a collection of statements and those statements have to be included inside the `<script>` tags.

```
first_script.html        ×    script.html           ×
1  <script>
2      //Javascript statements
3  </script>
4  |
```

JavaScript has to be invoked from another application such as a browser. Browsers have a built-in JavaScript engine that interprets and executes the JavaScript on the webpage. The interpretation of JavaScript is from top to bottom and goes from left to right. SpiderMonkey and Rhino are few of the early JavaScript engines that were implemented by different browsers, such as Netscape Navigator and Mozilla Firefox.

Next is our simple Hello World program; the JavaScript program is in between the `<script>` tags in the head section. The script tags can either be added to the head tag or to the body tag. As JavaScript is not non-blocking, the scripts hold the page until they are loaded. It is common to see the scripts being loaded at the end; this would work if there were no dependencies to other files or elements. One such example of a dependency would be a library that is used from a different location. We will be looking at a lot of these examples in the later chapters. We will be discussing the role of Unobtrusive JavaScript at a later point. For our Hello World program, use a text editor of your choice, and save this program with an HTML extension. Load the file in a web browser, and a pop-up box with the text **Hello World!** should be loaded on the page.

The following code snippet is the `first_script.html` file:

```html
<!DOCTYPE html>
<html>
    <head>
        <title>Test Javascript</title>
        <script type="text/javascript">
            alert("Hello World!");
        </script>
    </head>
    <body>
        <h2>First Script</h2>
        <p>This is a test program to alert Hello World!</p>
    </body>
</html>
```

The output is as follows:

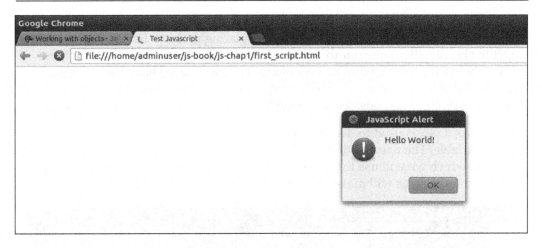

Variables in JavaScript

Now that we have built a Hello World program, let us take the next step and perform a few arithmetic operations on two numbers.

> The semi colon (;) is a statement terminator, it tells the JavaScript engine that a statement has ended.

Let us take a look at another program, `alert_script.html`:

```html
<!DOCTYPE html>
<html>
    <head>
        <title>Test Javascript</title>
        <script type="text/javascript">
            alert(5+3 );
            alert(5-3);
            alert(5*3);
            alert(5/3);
        </script>
    </head>
    <body>
        <h2>First Script</h2>
        <p>This is a test program to alert Hello World!</p>
    </body>
</html>
```

The previous program would run and produce four pop-up windows, one after the other, displaying their respective values. A glaring problem here is that we are repetitively using the same numbers in multiple places. If we had to perform these arithmetic operations on a different set of numbers, we would have had to replace them at multiple locations. To avoid this situation, we would assign those numbers to temporary storage locations; these storage locations are often referred to as variables.

The keyword `var` is used to declare a variable in JavaScript, followed by the name of that variable. The name is then implicitly provided with a piece of computer memory, which we will use throughout the program execution. Let us take a quick look at how variables will make the earlier program more flexible:

```
var.html
1  <html>
2      <head>
3          <script type="text/javascript">
4              var a = 5;
5              var b = 3;
6          </script>
7      </head>
8  </html>
```

Code commenting can be done in two ways: one is single line, and the other is multiline.

Single line comments:

```
//This program would alert the sum of 5 and 3;
alert(5+3);
```

Multiline comments:

```
/* This program would generate two alerts, the first
alert would display the sum of 5 and 3, and the second
alert would display the difference of 5 and 3 */
alert(5+3);
alert(5-3);
```

Let us continue with the program:

```
var_alert.html          x
1    <html>
2        <head>
3            <script type="text/javascript">
4                var a = 5;
5                var b = 3;
6
7                alert(a+b); //alerts 5+3
8                alert(a-b); //alerts 5-3
9                alert(a*b); //alerts 5*3
10               alert(a/b); //alerts 5/3
11
12           </script>
13       </head>
14   </html>
```

Now let us alter the value from 5 to 6; the amount of change that we will make here is minimal. We assign the value of 6 to our variable a, and that takes care of the rest of the process; unlike our earlier script where changes were made in multiple locations. This is shown as follows:

Code commenting is a recurring and an extremely important step in the development life cycle of any application. It has to be used to explain any assumptions and/or any dependencies that our code contains.

```
var_alert.html          x
1    <html>
2        <head>
3            <script type="text/javascript">
4                /*Let us alter the value of variable a to 6*/
5                var a = 6;
6                var b = 3;
7
8                alert(a+b); //alerts 6+3
9                alert(a-b); //alerts 6-3
10               alert(a*b); //alerts 6*3
11               alert(a/b); //alerts 6/3
12
13           </script>
14       </head>
15   </html>
```

In JavaScript, we declare a variable by using the keyword var and until a value is assigned to it, the value of the variable will be implicitly set to undefined; that value is overwritten on variable initialization.

Arrays

Variables are good to hold single values, but for cases where a variable should contain multiple values, we would have to rely on arrays. A JavaScript array is a collection of items arranged in an order, according to their index. Each item, in the array, is an element and has an index, which is used to access that element. Arrays are like a bookshelf that holds more than one book; each book having its unique location. Arrays are declared using the array literal notation [].

Let us look at a simple array declaration:

```
array_intro.html
1   <html>
2       <head>
3           <script type="text/javascript">
4               /*Arrays*/
5               |
6               var bookshelf = [];
7
8           </script>
9       </head>
10  </html>
```

 Arrays in JavaScript are zero based.

Let us initialize the array:

```
array_intro.html
1
2   var bookshelf = [];
3
4   bookshelf[0] = "book-1";
5   bookshelf[1] = "book-2";
6   .
7   .
8   .
9   bookshelf[n-1] = "book-n";
10
```

To access the value of a specific element, the reference index of that element is used. Once the reference index is identified, it can be outputted using the alert statement, as shown in the following screenshot:

```
array_intro.html      ●
1
2    alert(bookshelf[0]);|
3
```

Unlike variables, arrays are not typed, therefore, they can contain various types of data, as shown in the following screenshot:

```
array_intro.html      ●
1
2    var |exampleArray = ["John", 100, 200, 300, "Jane"];
3
```

A much more complex example of a JavaScript array is a multidimensional array, where there is a combination of arrays inside an array, as seen in the following screenshot:

```
array_intro.html      ●
1
2    var arrayOne = [1, 2, 3 ,4];
3    var arrayTwo = ["One", "Two", "Three", "Four"];
4    var multidimensionalArray = [arrayOne, arrayTwo] ;
5
```

To retrieve an element from a multidimensional array, we would have to use as many indexes as the levels in that array. If the multidimensional array contains an array that has the values that we want to access, we will have to choose the index where the array element exists, and then choose the index of the value inside the array that we are searching for. To retrieve the string Three from the multidimensionalArray example, we will have to first locate the index of the array containing the value Three, and then find the index of the value Three inside that array. This is shown as follows:

```
array_intro.html      ●
1
2    alert(multidimensionalArray[1][2]);
3
```

The second way of declaring an array is by using the `Array` class.

```
var bookshelf = new Array()
```

Objects

Objects are another way of handling data. In arrays the indexes are commonly numerical; objects give us a robust way of assigning and retrieving data. Objects are derived from the object-oriented programming concept; a programming paradigm that is very popular. Objects are a virtual representation of real-time data; they allow us to organize our data into logical groups via properties and methods. Properties describe the state of the object, while methods describe the behavior of the object. Properties are a key-value pair that holds the information. Take a look at the following:

```
object_intro.html    x
1   <html>
2       <head>
3           <script type="text/javascript">
4               /*Objects*/
5
6               var person = new Object();
7               person.firstname = "John";
8               person.lastname = "Doe";
9
10              person.getFullName = function(){
11                  alert(person.firstname+' '+person.lastname);
12              };
13
14              person.getFullName();
15
16          </script>
17      </head>
18  </html>
```

In the previous example, we have instantiated a `person` object, and then added the `firstname` and `lastname` properties that described the object. We added behavior to the object by creating a method called `getFullName`, the method accessed the object properties, retrieved the data, and alerted the output onto the screen. In this example the properties are accessed by the dot notation; we could also access a property by putting the property name in square brackets similar to an array, but it is not popular. This is shown as follows:

```
object_intro.html
1
2   alert(person["firstname"]);
3   |
```

The second way of creating an object is by using the curly braces. Here we are introduced to the `this` keyword, which provides a reference to the object's properties and methods, as shown in the following:

```
object_intro.html
1
2   var person = {
3           "firstname":"John",
4           "lastname":"Doe",
5           "getFullName": function(){
6                   alert(this.firstname+' '+this.lastname);
7               },
8           };
9
```

The Carousel application

We will be working on a Carousel application, which is powered by a JSON feed. We will be using HTML, JavaScript, and JSON to build this application. This application will have its very own navigation system coupled with a timer event in the background, which will rotate the items at a given interval. We will also be discussing how user experience plays an important role in developing such an application.

Summary

This chapter is a basic introduction to the principles of JavaScript that we will be utilizing in our journey towards mastering JSON. Variables, arrays, and objects play a very important role in carrying the data across the network. If this is your first encounter with JavaScript, go through the examples another time and practice them. We will need a strong foundation in order to build a solid understanding of JSON, and how it can be used in real-time web applications.

The Carousel application

Summary

2
Getting Started with JSON

JSON or JavaScript Object Notation is a very popular data interchange format. It was developed by Douglas Crockford. JSON is text-based, lightweight, and a human-readable format for data exchange between clients and servers. JSON is derived from JavaScript and bears a close resemblance to JavaScript objects, but it is not dependent on JavaScript. JSON is language-independent, and support for the JSON data format is available in all the popular languages, some of which are C#, PHP, Java, C++, Python, and Ruby.

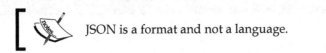
[JSON is a format and not a language.]

JSON can be used in web applications for data transfer. Prior to JSON, XML was considered to be the chosen data interchange format. XML parsing required an XML DOM implementation on the client side that would ingest the XML response, and then XPath was used to query the response in order to access and retrieve the data. That made life tedious, as querying for data had to be performed at two levels: first on the server side where the data was being queried from a database, and the second time was on the client side using XPath. JSON does not need any specific implementations; the JavaScript engine in the browser handles JSON parsing.

XML messages often tend to be heavy and verbose, and take up a lot of bandwidth while sending the data over a network connection. Once the XML message is retrieved, it has to be loaded into memory to parse it; let us take a look at a students data feed in XML and JSON.

The following is an example in XML:

```xml
1  <?xml version="1.0" encoding="UTF-8"?>
2  <!-- This is an example students feed in XML -->
3  <students>
4      <student>
5          <studentid>101</studentid>
6          <firstname>John</firstname>
7          <lastname>Doe</lastname>
8          <classes>
9              <class>Business Research</class>
10             <class>Economics</class>
11             <class>Finance</class>
12         </classes>
13     </student>
14     <student>
15         <studentid>102</studentid>
16         <firstname>Jane</firstname>
17         <lastname>Dane</lastname>
18         <classes>
19             <class>Marketing</class>
20             <class>Economics</class>
21             <class>Finance</class>
22         </classes>
23     </student>
24 </students>
25
```

Let us take a look at the example in JSON:

```json
1  /* This is an example students feed in JSON */
2  {
3      "students": {
4          "0": {
5              "studentid": "101",
6              "firstname": "John",
7              "lastname": "Doe",
8              "classes": [
9                  "Business Research",
10                 "Economics",
11                 "Finance"
12             ]
13         },
14         "1": {
15             "studentid": "102",
16             "firstname": "Jane",
17             "lastname": "Dane",
18             "class": [
19                 "Marketing",
20                 "Economics",
21                 "Finance"
22             ]
23         }
24     }
25 }
26
```

As we notice, the size of the XML message is bigger when compared to its JSON counterpart, and this is just for two records. A real-time feed will begin with a few thousands and go upwards. Another point to note is the amount of data that has to be generated by the server and then transmitted over the Internet is already big, and XML, as it is verbose, makes it bigger. Given that we are in the age of mobile devices where smart phones and tablets are getting more and more popular by the day, transmitting such large volumes of data on a slower network causes slow page loads, hang ups, and poor user experience, thus driving the users away from the site. JSON has come about to be the preferred Internet data interchange format, to avoid the issues mentioned earlier.

Since JSON is used to transmit serialized data over the Internet, we will need to make a note of its MIME type. A **MIME (Multipurpose Internet Mail Extensions)** type is an Internet media type, which is a two-part identifier for content that is being transferred over the Internet. The MIME types are passed through the HTTP headers of an HTTP Request and an HTTP Response. The MIME type is the communication of content type between the server and the browser. In general, a MIME type will have two or more parts that give the browser information about the type of data that is being sent either in the HTTP Request or in the HTTP Response. The MIME type for JSON data is `application/json`. If the MIME type headers are not sent across the browser, it treats the incoming JSON as plain text.

The Hello World program with JSON

Now that we have a basic understanding of JSON, let us work on our Hello World program. This is shown in the screenshot that follows:

```html
json_helloworld.html  x
1   <!DOCTYPE html>
2   <html>
3       <head>
4           <title>Test Javascript</title>
5           <script type="text/javascript">
6
7               var o = {"Hello":"World"};
8
9               alert(o.Hello);
10
11          </script>
12      </head>
13      <body>
14          <h2>JSON Hello World</h2>
15          <p>This is a test program to alert Hello World!</p>
16      </body>
17  </html>
18
```

The preceding program will alert World onto the screen when it is invoked from a browser. Let us pay close attention to the script between the `<script>` tags.

```
untitled
1
2   var hello_world = {"Hello":"World"};
3   alert(hello_world.Hello);
4   |
```

In the first step, we are creating a JavaScript variable and initializing the variable with a JavaScript object. Similar to how we retrieve data from a JavaScript object, we use the key-value pair to retrieve the value. Simply put, JSON is a collection of key and value pairs, where every key is a reference to the memory location where the value is stored on the computer. Now let us take a step back and analyze why we need JSON, if all we are doing is assigning JavaScript objects that are readily available. The answer is, JSON is a different format altogether, unlike JavaScript, which is a language.

 JSON keys and values have to be enclosed in double quotes, if either are enclosed in single quotes, we will receive an error.

Now, let us take a quick look at the similarities and differences between JSON and a normal JavaScript object. If we were to create a similar JavaScript object like our `hello_world` JSON variable from the earlier example, it would look like the JavaScript object that follows:

```
untitled
1
2   var hello_world = {Hello: "World"};
```

The big difference here is that the key is not wrapped in double quotes. Since a JSON key is a string, we can use any valid string for a key. We can use spaces, special characters, and hyphens in our keys, which is not valid in a normal JavaScript object.

```
untitled
1
2   var hello_world = {"test-hello":"World"};|
```

When we use special characters, hyphens, or spaces in our keys, we have to be careful while accessing them.

```
untitled
1
2   alert(hello_world.test-hello); //doesn't work
```

The reason the preceding JavaScript statement doesn't work is that JavaScript doesn't accept keys with special characters, hyphens, or strings. So we have to retrieve the data using a method where we will handle the JSON object as an associative array with a string key. This is shown in the screenshot that follows:

```
untitled
1
2   alert(hello_world["test-hello"]); //hurray!! It works
```

Another difference between the two is that a JavaScript object can carry functions within, while a JSON object cannot carry any functions. The example that follows has the property getName, which has a function that alerts the name John Doe when it is invoked:

```
untitled
1
2   {
3       "id":101,
4       "name": "John Doe",
5       "isStudent": true,
6
7
8       "scores" : [10, 20, 30, 40],
9       "courses" : {
10              "major":"Finance",
11              "minor": "Marketing"
12      }
13  }
14  
```

Finally, the biggest difference is that a JavaScript object was never intended to be a data interchange format, while the sole purpose of JSON was to use it as a data interchange format.

Datatypes in JSON

Now, let us take a look at a more complex example of JSON. We'll also go over all the datatypes that are supported by JSON. JSON supports six datatypes: strings, numbers, Booleans, arrays, objects, and null.

```
untitled
1
2   var javascriptObject = {
3        id : 101,
4        name: "John Doe",
5        getName : function(){
6            alert(this.name);
7        }
8   }
9
```

In the preceding example, we have five key-value pairs of different datatypes. Now let us take a close look at each of these key-value pairs:

```
untitled
1
2   "id":101
3
```

The datatype of the value that `"id"` references is a number.

```
untitled
1
2   "name":"John Doe"
3
```

Here, the datatype of the value that `"name"` references is a string.

```
untitled
1
2   "isStudent": true
3
```

In the preceding screenshot, the datatype of the value that `"isStudent"` references is a Boolean.

```
untitled
1
2  "scores" : [10, 20, 30, 40]
3
```

The datatype of the value that `"scores"` references here is an array.

```
untitled
1
2  "courses" : {
3            "major":"Finance",
4            "minor":"Marketing"
5  }
6
```

Here the datatype of the value that `"courses"` references is an object.

We know that JSON supports six datatypes; they are strings, numbers, Booleans, arrays, objects, and null. Yes, JSON supports null data, and real-time business implementations need accurate information. There might be cases where null was substituted with an empty string, but that is inaccurate. Let us take a quick look at the following example:

```
untitled
1
2  var nullVal = "";
3
4  alert(typeof nullVal); //prints string
5
6  var nullVal = null;
7
8  alert(typeof nullVal); //prints object
9
```

 Arrays and null values are objects in JavaScript.

In the earlier example, we are using the `typeof` operator that takes an operand, and returns the datatype of that operand. On line 4, we are determining the type of an empty string, while on line 8 we are determining the type of a null value.

Now, let us implement our JSON object in a page and retrieve the values, as shown in the following screenshot:

```
json_data.html

1   <html>
2        <head>
3              <script type="text/javascript">
4                   var complexJson = {
5                        "id": 101,
6                        "name": "John Doe",
7                        "isStudent": true,
8                        "scores": [
9                             10,
10                            20,
11                            30,
12                            40
13                        ],
14                        "courses": {
15                             "major": "Finance",
16                             "minor": "Marketing"
17                        }
18                   }
19
20              </script>
21        </head>
22        <body>
23              <h2>Complex Data in JSON</h2>
24              <p>This is a test program to load complex json data into a variable</p>
25        </body>
26   </html>
27
```

To retrieve the `id` from the variable `complexJson`, we need to do the following:

```
untitled

1
2   alert(complexJson.id); //alerts 101
3
```

To retrieve the `name` from the variable `complexJson`, look at the screenshot that is shown:

```
untitled

1
2   alert(complexJson.name); //alerts John Doe
3
```

Look at the following screenshot to retrieve `isStudent` from the variable `complexJson`:

```
untitled                    ●
1
2   alert(complexJson.isStudetn); //alerts true
3
```

Retrieving data from arrays and objects gets a little tricky, as we have to traverse through the array or object. Let us see how values can be retrieved from arrays:

```
untitled                    ●
1
2   var complexJson = {
3                   "id": 101,
4                   "name": "John Doe",
5                   "isStudent": true,
6                   "scores": [
7                   |   10,
8                       20,
9                       30,
10                      40
11                  ],
12                  "courses": {
13                      "major": "Finance",
14                      "minor": "Marketing"
15                  }
16              }
17
18
19   alert(complexJson.scores[1]); //alerts 102
20
```

In the preceding example, we are retrieving the second element from the `scores` array. Although `scores` is an array inside the `complexJson` object, it is still treated as a regular key-value pair. It is handled differently when the key is accessed; the first thing that the interpreter has to assess, when a key is accessed, is to get the datatype of its value. If the retrieved value is a string, number, Boolean, or null, there will not be any extra operations that are performed on the value. But if it is an array or an object, the value's dependencies are taken into consideration.

To retrieve an element from the object inside a JSON object, we will have to access the key that is the reference for that value, as shown:

```
untitled
1
2  alert(complexJson.courses.major); //alerts "Finance"
3
```

Since objects do not have a numeric index, JavaScript might rearrange the order of items inside an object. If you notice that the order of key-value pairs during the initialization of the JSON object is different from when you are accessing the data, there is nothing to worry about. There is no loss of data; the JavaScript engine has just reordered your object.

Languages that support JSON

Until now, we have seen how the parsers in JavaScript support JSON. There are many other programming languages that provide implementations for JSON. Languages such as PHP, Python, C#, C++, and Java provide a very good support for the JSON data interchange format. All of the popular programming languages that support service-oriented architecture have understood the importance of JSON and its implementation for data transfer, thus, they have provided great support for JSON. Let us take a quick detour from implementing JSON in JavaScript, and see how JSON is implemented in other languages, such as PHP and Python.

PHP

PHP is considered to be one of the most popular languages for building web applications. It is a server-side scripting language that allows developers to build applications that can perform operations on the server, connect to a database to perform CRUD (Create, Read, Update, Delete) operations, and provide a stately environment for real-time applications. JSON support has been built into the PHP core from PHP 5.2.0; this helps users avoid going through any complex installations or configurations. Given that JSON is just a data interchange format, PHP consists of two functions. These functions handle JSON that comes in via a request or generate JSON that will be sent via a response. PHP is a weakly-typed language; for this example, we will use the data stored in a PHP array and convert that data into a JSON string, which can be utilized as a data feed. Let us recreate the student example that we have used in an earlier section, build it in PHP, and convert it into JSON.

This example is only intended to show you how JSON can be generated using PHP.

```php
json_encode.php    x
1   <?php
2
3   $student = array("id"=>101,
4                    "name"=>"John Doe",
5                    "isStudent"=>true,
6                    "scores"=>array(10, 20, 30, 40),
7                    "courses" => array(
8                        "major"=>"Finance",
9                        "minor"=>"Marketing"
10                       )
11         );
12
13  echo json_encode($student); //encoding the array into a JSON string
14                              //and using echo to  print the output
15
16  ?>
17
```

To run a PHP script, we will need to install PHP. To run a PHP script through a browser, we will need a web server, such as Apache or IIS. We will go through the installation in *Chapter 4, AJAX Calls with JSON Data*, when we work with AJAX.

This script starts by initializing a variable, and assigning an associative array that contains student information. The variable $students is then passed to a function called json_encode(), which converts the variable into a JSON string. When this script is run, it generates a valid response that can be exposed as a JSON data feed for other applications to utilize.

The output is as follows:

```
untitled
1
2  {
3      "id":101,"name":"John Doe","isStudent":true,
4      "scores":[10,20,30,40],
5      "courses":{"major":"Finance","minor":"Marketing"}
6  }
7
```

We have successfully generated our first JSON feed via a simple PHP script; let us take a look at the method to parse JSON that comes in via an HTTP request. It is common for web applications that make asynchronous HTTP requests to send data in JSON format.

 This example is only intended to show you how JSON can be ingested into PHP.

```php
json_decode.php    x
1   <?php
2
3   //json string from a HTTP request
4
5   $student = '{"id":101,"name":"John Doe","isStudent":true,"scores":[10,20,30,40],
6               "courses":{"major":"Finance","minor":"Marketing"}}';
7
8   print_r(json_decode($student, true)); //decoding a JSON string
9                                         //and converting it into a PHP array
10
11  ?>
```

The output is as follows:

```
untitled                 *
1
2   Array
3   (
4       [id] => 101
5       [name] => John Doe
6       [isStudent] => 1
7       [scores] => Array
8           (
9               [0] => 10
10              [1] => 20
11              [2] => 30
12              [3] => 40
13          )
14
15      [courses] => Array
16          (
17              [major] => Finance
18              [minor] => Marketing
19          )
20  )
21
```

Python

Python is a very popular scripting language that is extensively used to perform string operations and to build console applications. It can be used to fetch data from a JSON API, and once the JSON data is retrieved it will be treated as a JSON string. To perform any operations on that JSON string, Python provides the JSON module. The JSON module is an amalgamation of many powerful functions that we can use to parse the JSON string on hand.

 This example is only intended to show you how JSON can be generated using Python.

```
json_dumps.py          ×
1   #! /usr/bin/python
2
3   import json
4
5   student = [{'id':101, 'name':'John Doe', 'isStudent':True,
6               'scores':(10, 20, 30, 40),
7               'courses':{'major':'Finance', 'minor':'Marketing'}
8               }]
9
10  print json.dumps(student)
11
```

In this example we have used complex datatypes, such as Tuples and Dictionaries, to store the scores and courses respectively; since this is not a Python course, we will not go deep into those datatypes.

 To run this script Python2 needs to be installed, it comes preinstalled on any *nix operating system.

The output is as follows:

```
untitled                ●
1
2   [{
3       "isStudent": true,
4       "courses": {"major": "Finance", "minor": "Marketing"},
5       "scores": [10, 20, 30, 40],
6       "id": 101, "name": "John Doe"
7   }]
8
```

The keys might get rearranged based on the datatype; we can use the sort_keys flag to retrieve the original order.

Now, let us take a quick look at how the JSON decoding is performed in Python.

 This example is only intended to show you how JSON can be ingested into Python.

```python
json_loads.py                    x
1  #!/usr/bin/python
2
3  import json
4
5  student_json = '''[{"isStudent": true,
6                    "courses": {"major": "Finance", "minor": "Marketing"},
7                    "scores": [10, 20, 30, 40], "id": 101,
8                    "name": "John Doe"}]'''
9
10 print json.loads(student_json);
11
```

In this example, we are storing the JSON string in student_json, and we are using the json.loads() method that is available through the JSON module in Python.

The output is as follows:

```
[{
1  [{
2      u'isStudent': True,
3      u'courses': {u'major': u'Finance', u'minor': u'Marketing'},
4      u'id': 101,
5      u'name': u'John Doe',
6      u'scores': [10, 20, 30, 40]
7  }]
8
```

Summary

This chapter introduced us to the basics of JSON. We went through the history of JSON, and understood its advantages over XML. We created our first JSON object and successfully parsed it. Also, we went over all the datatypes that JSON supports. Finally, we went over some examples as to how JSON can be implemented in other programming languages. As we move forward in this journey, we will find the knowledge that we have gathered in this chapter to be a solid foundation for the more complex concepts that we will go over in the later chapters.

3

Working with Real-time JSON

In the previous chapter, I introduced you to basic JSON, how JSON objects can be embedded into an HTML file, and how basic operations such as accessing keys can be performed on simple JSON objects. Now let us take a step forward and work with JSON objects that are bigger, more complex, and closer to the JSON that we would work with in real-time situations. In real-world applications, JSON can be retrieved either as a response from an asynchronous request or from a JSON feed. A website uses HTML, CSS, and JavaScript to provide a visually beautiful user interface. But there are cases where data vendors are only focused on getting the data. A **data feed** serves their purpose; a feed is a crude way of supplying data so that others can reuse it to display the data on their websites or to ingest the data and run their algorithms on it. Such data feeds are big in size and cannot directly be embedded into the `script` tag. Let us look at how external JavaScript files can be included in an HTML file.

The following screenshot depicts the code for the `external-js.html` file:

```
external-js.html    x    example.js    x
1   <!DOCTYPE html>
2   <html>
3       <head>
4           <title>Include External Javascript</title>
5           <script type="text/javascript" src="example.js"></script>
6           <script type="text/javascript">
7
8               alert(x);
9
10          </script>
11      </head>
12      <body>
13          <h2>Include External JavaScript</h2>
14          <p>This is a test program to learn how external
15                          javascript files can be included.</p>
16      </body>
17  </html>
18
```

In this example, we include `example.js`, which is an external JavaScript file.

```
external-js.html    x    example.js    •
1
2   var x = "This is the value of variable x and is being retrieved
3                           |from an external javascript file";
4
```

To access the variable x that is in the `example.js` file from the `external-js.html` file, we write our programs within our `script` tags in the HTML file.

This file has to be created in the same folder as `external-js.html`. Follow the given folder structure:

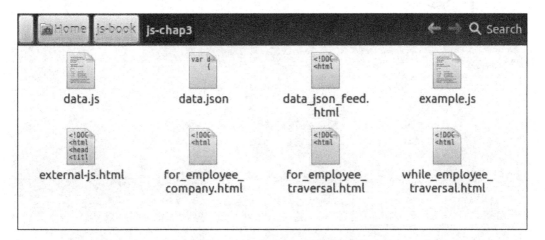

Accessing objects in JSON

Now that we understand how to make a script call to fetch an external JavaScript file, let us use the same technique to import a JSON feed. I have generated a test `employee` JSON data feed with 100 records. To traverse through any JSON feed, it is important to make a note of how the data is arranged. The keys in this data feed are basic employee information such as employee number, date of birth, first name, last name, gender, hire date, titles that they have held, and the dates during which they have held those titles. A few employees have held the same title throughout their tenure, while there are some employees who have held more than one title.

This JSON file will be part of the code files for exercises.

```
data.js                    x
 1  var data_json = [
 2      {
 3          "emp_no": "10001",
 4          "birth_date": "1953-09-02",
 5          "first_name": "Georgi",
 6          "last_name": "Facello",
 7          "gender": "M",
 8          "hire_date": "1986-06-26",
 9          "titles": {
10              "title": "Senior Engineer",
11              "from_date": "1986-06-26",
12              "to_date": "9999-01-01"
13          }
14      },
15      {
16          "emp_no": "10002",
17          "birth_date": "1964-06-02",
18          "first_name": "Bezalel",
19          "last_name": "Simmel",
20          "gender": "F",
21          "hire_date": "1985-11-21",
22          "titles": {
23              "title": "Staff",
24              "from_date": "1996-08-03",
25              "to_date": "9999-01-01"
26          }
27      },
28      {
29          "emp_no": "10003",
30          "birth_date": "1959-12-03",
31          "first_name": "Parto",
32          "last_name": "Bamford",
33          "gender": "M",
```

As we are dealing with a complex JSON data feed, let us save the data feed to a file. In the data_json_feed.html file, we have imported the data.json file, which is in the same folder as the HTML file. It is noteworthy that the JSON feed has been assigned to a variable called data_json, and to access the JSON feed, we will have to use this variable in the data_json_feed.html file:

```
data.json              ×      data_json_feed.html ×
1   <!DOCTYPE html>
2   <html>
3       <head>
4           <title>Include Extenal JSON Feed</title>
5           <script type="text/javascript" src="data.json"></script>
6           <script type="text/javascript">
7
8               console.log(data_json);
9
10          </script>
11      </head>
12      <body>
13          <h2>Include External JSON</h2>
14          <p>This is a test program to learn how external JSON
15              feed stored in files can be included.</p>
16      </body>
17  </html>
18
```

Another thing to note is the use of a new method called `console.log`. Browsers such as Mozilla Firefox, Google Chrome, and Apple Safari profile a console panel for run-time JavaScript development and debugging. The use of the JavaScript function `alert` is discouraged due to its obtrusive behavior. `console.log`, on the other hand, is unobtrusive and logs its messages to the console. From here on, we will refrain from using the `alert` method and will use `console.log` to print data into the console window. Google Chrome and Apple Safari come with developer tools already installed; to view the console, right-click on the page and click on **Inspect Element**. Both of them come with a **Console** tab that allows us to work with our logging. Firefox is dependent on Firebug; in *Chapter 8, Debugging JSON*, I will walk you through the installation steps of Firebug.

```
                    Console  HTML  CSS  Script  DOM ▼  Net                    ⌕

window > Object

  ⊞ 10001           Object { emp_no="10001",  birth_date="1953-09-02",  first_name="Georgi",  more... }
  ⊞ 10002           Object { emp_no="10002",  birth_date="1964-06-02",  first_name="Bezalel",  more... }
  ⊞ 10003           Object { emp_no="10003",  birth_date="1959-12-03",  first_name="Parto",  more... }
  ⊞ 10004           Object { emp_no="10004",  birth_date="1954-05-01",  first_name="Chirstian",
                    more... }
  ⊞ 10005           Object { emp_no="10005",  birth_date="1955-01-21",  first_name="Kyoichi",  more... }
  ⊞ 10006           Object { emp_no="10006",  birth_date="1953-04-20",  first_name="Anneke",  more... }
  ⊞ 10007           Object { emp_no="10007",  birth_date="1957-05-23",  first_name="Tzvetan",  more... }
  ⊞ 10008           Object { emp_no="10008",  birth_date="1958-02-19",  first_name="Saniya",  more... }
  ⊞ 10009           Object { emp_no="10009",  birth_date="1952-04-19",  first_name="Sumant",  more... }
  ⊞ 10010           Object { emp_no="10010",  birth_date="1963-06-01",  first_name="Duangkaew",
                    more... }
  ⊞ 10011           Object { emp_no="10011",  birth_date="1953-11-07",  first_name="Mary",  more... }
  ⊞ 10012           Object { emp_no="10012",  birth_date="1960-10-04",  first_name="Patricio",
                    more... }
  ⊞ 10013           Object { emp_no="10013",  birth_date="1963-06-07",  first_name="Eberhardt",
                    more... }
  ⊞ 10014           Object { emp_no="10014",  birth_date="1956-02-12",  first_name="Berni",  more... }
```

When we load the `data_json_feed.html` file into the Firefox browser, open up our console window, and click on the **DOM** tab, we are going to see a list of 100 `employee` objects. If our object is small and has one or two child objects, we would prefer using their numeric indexes to access them; in this case, as we have a huge number of child objects, it is not realistic to target objects based on static indexes.

```
untitled
1
2  Ex: console.log(employees[10003].emp_no); //Not realistic,
3                              //unless we are targeting a specific key.
4
```

Performing complex operations

To tackle an array of objects, we have to handle them in an iterative method. We will have to come up with an iterative solution in which we target one object at a time; once the object is accessed, we would not target that object another time. This allows us to maintain data integrity as we can avoid accessing the same object multiple times, thereby avoiding any redundancies. The looping statements in JavaScript are the `while` loop and the `for` loop. Let us take a quick look at how we can use these looping techniques to traverse through our employees' array.

```
data_json_feed.html x    while_employee_traversal.html
4          <title>Parse JSON Feed using While</title>
5          <script type="text/javascript" src="data.js"></script>
6          <script type="text/javascript">
7
8                  var i = 0;
9                  var employeeCount = data_json.length;
10
11                 while(i<employeeCount){
12
13                         console.log("Employee number is "+data_json[i].emp_no);
14                         i++;
15                 }
16
17          </script>
18      </head>
19      <body>
20          <h2>Parse JSON Feed using While</h2>
21          <p>This is a test program to learn how external JSON
22          feed stored in files can be parsed using the While Loop.</p>
23      </body>
24  </html>
25
```

In the `while_employees_traversal.html` file, we are importing the `data.js` file, which we had examined in the previous section. The `data_json` variable inside the `data.js` file consists of an array of objects that are imported into this HTML page. In the `script` tags, we are setting up two variables: the `i` variable to hold a starting counter and the `employeeCount` variable to hold the counter of the total number of objects in `data_json`. To retrieve the number of items that exists in an array, we can use the `.length` property that is provided by JavaScript. There are three important supporting blocks for a `while` loop: the condition, statements in the `while` loop, and either the increment or decrement operation based on the condition. Let us take a quick look at these three separately:

```
untitled                    *
1
2   while(i<employeeCount) //the condition is inside the bracket
3
```

We are initializing the variable `i` to zero and the condition that we are looking for is if zero is less than the number of items in the variable `data_json`, then proceed into the loop.

```
untitled                    *
1
2   //statements within the while loop
3   console.log("Employee number is "+data_json[i].emp_no);
4
```

If the condition is true, the statements inside the loop are executed, until they hit the incrementing condition:

```
untitled                    *
1
2   //increment or decrement based on the condition
3
4   i++; //use i-- for decrementing
5
```

Once the incrementing operator approaches, the value of the i variable is incremented by 1, and it will go back to the initial step of the while loop. At the initial step, the condition is again verified to check if i is still less than the number of items in data_json. If that were true, it would again enter the loop and execute the statements. This process continues to repeat itself until the value of variable i is equal to that of employeeCount. At that point, the while loop's execution is complete, and the statements inside the while loop are maintained as logs in the console window of the browser. Before running the HTML file, while_employees_traversal.html, verify that the data.json file is in the same directory as the HTML file. Load this HTML file into a browser of your choice (Chrome, Firefox, or Safari are recommended), open up the console window by right-clicking on the web page and clicking on **Inspect Element** if you are on Chrome or Safari. The employee numbers should be displayed on the console window:

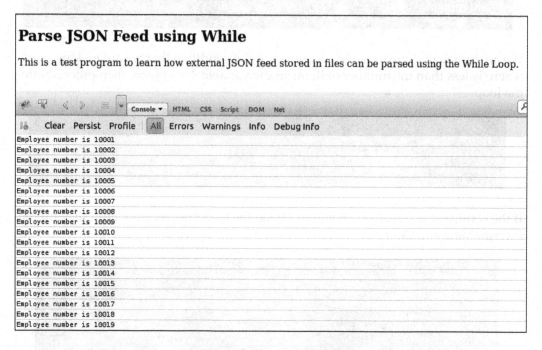

To retrieve the employee's first name and last name, we will concatenate the first_name and last_name keys in the employee object:

```
//To retrieve the Employee's full name

console.log("Employee's full Name is "+data_json[i].first_name+' '+data_json[i].last_name);
```

We can use the same technique to retrieve the rest of the keys such as `birth_date`, `gender`, and `hire_date`, except for `titles`. A quick glance at the JSON feed explains that unlike the rest of the keys, `titles` is an object or an array of objects. The `titles` object contains all the titles that the employee has held since joining the company. Some employees have one title, while others have more than one; so the former would be an object by itself, while the latter would be an array of objects, each containing a `title` object. To handle this case, we would have to check if the employee has one title or more than one title. If the person has one title, we should print the data, and if the person has more than one title, we would have to iterate them through the array of `title` objects to print all the titles that the employee has.

```
while_employee_traversal.html  x      untitled

var i = 0;
var employeeCount = data_json.length;

while(i<employeeCount){
        if(data_json[i].titles instanceof Array){
                //there are more than one titles for this employee
                var j=0
                var titleCount = data_json[i].titles.length;
                var titles = "";

                while(j<titleCount){
                        titles += data_json[i].titles[j].title+ " & ";
                        j++;
                }

                titles = titles.slice(0, titles.length-3);

                console.log("Employee "+ data_json[i].emp_no +" has served as "+titles);


        }
        else{
                //there is only one title for this employee
                var title = data_json[i].titles.title;
                console.log("Employee "+ data_json[i].emp_no +" has served as "+title);
        }

        i++;
}
```

The existent code in the `script` tags has to be replaced with the previous code, provided to retrieve the titles of the employee. In this script, we are using the variables `i` and `employeeCount` from our earlier script. We have introduced a new condition to check if the `titles` key for a particular employee is an `Array` object. This condition gets the type of the value that the loop is passing in and verifies if it is an instance of an `Array` object. Let us identify this condition that is checking the instance type:

```
if(data_json[i].titles instanceof Array)
```

Once this condition is satisfied, the statements inside the condition are executed. Inside the success condition we declare three variables. The first variable, `j`, would hold the counter for the second `while` loop that would iterate through `titles`. The second variable is `titleCount`; it would store the number of items that are available in the `titles` array. The last variable is `titles`, which is initialized to an empty string. This variable would hold all the titles held by the employee. It stores the list of titles as a list separated by `&`:

```
while(j<titleCount){
        titles += data_json[i].titles[j].title+ " & ";
        j++;
}
```

In this `while` loop, the titles of the employee are being built; one title at a time is being added to the `titles` variable. Once the title has been added to the `titles` variable, the value of `j` is incremented and the loop continues until all the `title` objects are iterated. If the `titles` key is not an array, the execution would go into the `else` block and the statements in the `else` block are executed. As there is only one title for that employee, the data would be directly printed onto the console. Now let us look at the same example and use the `for` loop. Similar to the `while` loop, the `for` loop also traverses through the array of employees from the `data_json` variable. The business logic remains the same irrespective of what looping technique is used. Let us re-create the same example using the `for` loop:

```
for_employee_traversal.html  x      untitled

for(var i in data_json){

        var data = data_json[i];
        if(data.titles instanceof Array){
            var titles = "";
            for(var j in data.titles){

                titles += data.titles[j].title + " & ";

            }

        titles = titles.slice(0, titles.length-3);
        console.log("Employee "+ data.emp_no +" has served as "+titles);
    }
    else{
        var title = data.titles.title;
        console.log("Employee "+ data.emp_no +" has served as "+title);
    }
}
```

Unlike the `while` loop, we would not need extra counter variables to hold the current index and the length of the array, the `for` loop takes care of those counters. Other than the foundational changes with the syntax, the business logic remains the same, as I had pointed out earlier. Now that we are familiar with how we can access objects and perform complex operations to extract data, in the next section, let us take a look at how JSON data can be modified.

Modifying JSON

JSON retrieved from a JSON feed is always going to be read-only; as such data feeds do not provide functionality to modify their data from unverified sources. There are many cases where we would want to ingest the data from an external data feed, and then modify that content as per our requirements. An example is a company that is using a data feed that is being supplied by a data vendor, but the data that is being provided is a lot more than the company requires. In such cases, rather than using the whole feed, the company would only extract a part of it, perform certain operations to modify it as per their requirements, and reuse the new JSON object. Let us take our `employee` JSON feed. Assume that the name of the company was different during different periods. We want to group the employees by company name, which is based on when they joined. Employees who joined the company before 1987 belong to Company 1 and those who joined the company in 1987 or after belong to Company 2. To represent this change, we add the `company` key to our JSON feed:

```
for_employee_company.html  ×
1   <!DOCTYPE html>
2   <html>
3       <head>
4           <title>Modifying JSON based on joining year</title>
5           <script type="text/javascript" src="data.json"></script>
6           <script type="text/javascript">
7
8               for(var i in data_json){
9
10                  var data = data_json[i];
11                  var join_year = parseInt(data.hire_date.slice(0,4));
12
13                  if(join_year < 1987){
14                      data.company = "Company1";
15                  }
16                  else{
17                      data.company = "Company2";
18                  }
19
20                  var message = "Employee "+data.emp_no+
21                      " joined in the year "+join_year+
22                      " belongs to "+data.company;
23
24                  console.log(message);
25              }
26
27          </script>
28      </head>
29      <body>
30          <h2>Modifying JSON based on joining year</h2>
31          <p>This is a test program to learn how JSON imported from a feed
32              could be locally modified.</p>
33      </body>
34  </html>
```

In the `for_employee_company.html` file, we are traversing through the array of `employee` objects and we are extracting the year in which the employee joined. We are converting this from a string to an integer, so we can use the year value for comparison purposes. We assign the parsed year to the `join_year` variable:

```
for_employee_company.html  ×     untitled
1
2   var data = data_json[i];
3
4   //retrieving the year
5   var join_year = parseInt(data.hire_date.slice(0,4));
6
```

In the following screenshot, we are checking to see if the employee joined the company before 1987; if they have joined before 1987, we add the `company` property to the `employee` object and assign the value of `Company1`. If they have joined in 1987 or after 1987, we assign the value of `Company2`:

```
for_employee_company.html  ×     untitled
1
2   if(join_year < 1987){
3           data.company = "Company1";
4   }
5   else{
6           data.company = "Company2";
7   }
8   |
```

After a value is assigned to the newly added property company, we build a generic message that would apply for all the employees, irrespective of which company they belong to. We extract the employee number, the year in which the employee joined, and the name of the company to generate that message:

```
for_employee_company.html  ×     untitled
1
2   var message = "Employee " + data.emp_no + " joined in the year " + join_year +
3           " belongs to "+data.company;
4
5   console.log(message);
6
```

When `for_employee_company.html` is run from the web browser, the script to perform the modifications is run and the output is logged to the console:

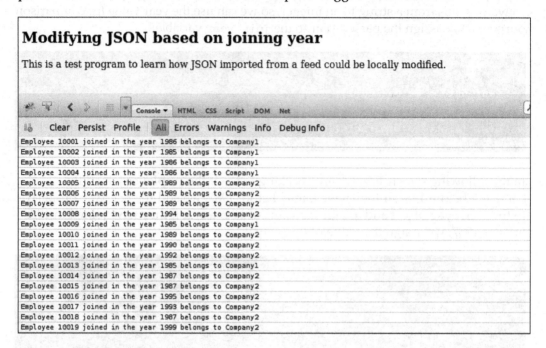

Summary

This chapter addresses the core concepts of how to handle static JSON feeds. We began by importing an external JSON object into our HTML file, looped through the complex array of objects to parse and extract required data. We used the `while` and `for` loops to loop through the array and used conditions to target our search. We completed this chapter by locally modifying the existing JSON feed and adding a new property, the `employee` object. Now that we have mastered accessing JSON from a static file, it is time for us to make some asynchronous calls to fetch some active JSON over HTTP.

4
AJAX Calls with JSON Data

JSON is considered today to be the most popular data interchange format. In the previous chapter we saw an example using a JSON feed as a data store. In this chapter let's make the data a little more dynamic. HTML, client-side JavaScript, and CSS provide the structural, behavioral, and presentational aspects respectively. Dynamic web development is all about data transfer between two parties, the client and the server. We use programs such as a web server, a database, and a server-side programming language to fetch and store dynamic data. Let's take a look at the process behind the scenes that facilitates successful operations on the data.

When a user opens up a web browser and types `http://www.packtpub.com/`, the browser makes a request to the **Internet Service Provider (ISP)** to perform a reverse lookup of the IP address by providing the domain name. Once the IP address is retrieved, the request is then forwarded to the machine that owns the IP address. At that point, there is a web server that is waiting to consume the request; the web server could be one of the top web servers, such as Apache, IIS, Tomcat, and Nginx. The web server receives the request and looks at the headers that are part of the HTTP request; those headers pass the information about the request that was made to the web server. Once the web server parses those headers, it routes the request over to a server-side programming application that is responsible for handling this request. The application could be written in PHP, C#/ASP.NET, Java/JSP, and so on. This responsible server-side language takes the request, understands it, and performs the necessary business logic to complete the request. A few examples of such HTTP requests are loading a web page and clicking the **Contact us** link on a website. There can be complex HTTP requests too, where the data has to be validated, cleansed, and/or retrieved from a data storage application such as a database, a file server, or a caching server.

These HTTP requests can be made in two ways—synchronously and asynchronously. A synchronous request is a blocking request, where everything has to be done in an orderly fashion, one step after another, and where the following step has to wait until the previous one has completed execution. Let's assume that there are four independent components on a web page when the page is loaded; if one component takes a long time during execution, the rest of the page is going to wait for it until its execution is complete. If execution fails, the page load fails too. One other example is when there is a poll and a ratings component on the web page; if the user chooses to answer the poll and give a rating to fulfill these requests, two requests have to be sent out one after the other if we go with a synchronous requesting mechanism.

To tackle the issue of synchronous requests, the development community has gradually made progress in the field of asynchronous HTTP requests. The first product to come out that allowed asynchronous requests were the IFrame tags, introduced by Microsoft; they used IFrames via Internet Explorer to load content asynchronously. After IFrame, next in line to revolutionize the Internet was the XML HTTP ActiveX control. In later years, all the browsers adopted this control under the new name XMLHTTPRequest JavaScript object, which is part of the XMLHTTPRequest API. The XMLHTTPRequest API is used to make an HTTP (or HTTPS) call to a web server. It can be used to make both synchronous and asynchronous calls. Asynchronous requests allow developers to divide web pages into multiple components independent of each other, thereby saving a lot of memory by sending data on demand.

Jesse James Garrett named this phenomenon "AJAX". In **AJAX (Asynchronous JavaScript and XML)**, web requests are made via JavaScript and the data interchange originally happened in XML. The "X" in AJAX was originally considered to be XML, but today it can be any data interchange format, such as XML, JSON, text file, or even HTML. The data format being used for the data transfer has to be mentioned in the MIME type headers. In *Chapter 2, Getting Started with JSON*, we have already highlighted why JSON is the preferred data interchange format. Let us take a quick look at what we would need to make our first AJAX call with JSON data.

Essentially, web developers can use the principles of AJAX to fetch data on demand to make websites more responsive and interactive; it is very important to understand what generates that demand. The trigger for such a demand for data is commonly an event that occurs on the web page. An **event** can be described as a reaction to an action that was performed, for example, ringing a bell produces a vibration inside the bell that generates the sound. Here, ringing a bell is the event, while the sound that is produced is the reaction to the event. There can be multiple events on a web page; a few such events are clicking a button, submitting a form, hovering over a link, and choosing an option from a drop-down, all of which are very common events. We have to come up with a way in which they are programmatically handled when these events occur.

Requirements for AJAX

AJAX is an asynchronous two-way communication between the browser that is considered to be the client, and a live web server via HTTP (or HTTPS). We can run a live server locally, such as Apache or IIS on Windows or Apache on Linux and Mac OS. I will take us through setting up the Apache web server in a Linux environment and simultaneously also explain how to use the Microsoft Visual Studio development environment to build web applications. For this AJAX course, let us pick PHP and MySQL to be our main server-side language and database.

In this chapter, I will take you through two setups; the first will be setting up Apache and PHP to develop server-side programs on a Linux machine, while the second one will be running a .NET-powered web application on Windows. Microsoft's .NET Framework requires the libraries in the .NET Framework and Visual Studio IDE to be installed. I will assume that you have performed both the steps; we will now set up a web application in ASP.NET, powered by C#.

Linux is an open source operating system and has been the chosen OS by the development fraternity for non-Microsoft programming and scripting languages, such as PHP, Python, Java, and Ruby. The development environment when using PHP, Perl, or Python on a Linux operating system is often referred to as a LAMP environment. **LAMP** stands for **Linux**, **Apache**, **MySQL**, and **PHP** (or **Python** or **Perl**). The `tasksel` package allows us to install Apache, MySQL, and PHP in a single shot. Let's take a quick look at the necessary steps for installing the LAMP stack. On your Linux operating system, open up the terminal and type `sudo apt-get install tasksel`. The operating system, based on your user privileges, might prompt you for a password; after entering the password, hit *Enter*.

```
File  Edit  View  Terminal  Go  Help
root@adminuser-1204-xbuntu:~#
root@adminuser-1204-xbuntu:~#
root@adminuser-1204-xbuntu:~#
root@adminuser-1204-xbuntu:~#
root@adminuser-1204-xbuntu:~#
root@adminuser-1204-xbuntu:~# sudo apt-get install tasksel
Reading package lists... Done
Building dependency tree
Reading state information... Done
The following extra packages will be installed:
    aptitude libapt-pkg4.12 libboost-iostreams1.46.1 libclass-accessor-perl libcwidget3 libept1.4.12 libio-string-per
    libsigc++-2.0-0c2a libsub-name-perl tasksel-data
Suggested packages:
    aptitude-doc-en aptitude-doc debtags libcwidget-dev libxml-simple-perl
The following NEW packages will be installed:
    aptitude libapt-pkg4.12 libboost-iostreams1.46.1 libclass-accessor-perl libcwidget3 libept1.4.12 libio-string-per
    libsigc++-2.0-0c2a libsub-name-perl tasksel tasksel-data
0 upgraded, 12 newly installed, 0 to remove and 859 not upgraded.
Need to get 2,510 kB/4,032 kB of archives.
After this operation, 12.9 MB of additional disk space will be used.
Do you want to continue [Y/n]?
```

As we are installing a package on the operating system, the OS will display the package and dependency information for the package it is installing and will prompt the user to check whether this is the targeted package. Hit the *Y* key on your keyboard to say "yes"; the operating system will then go to the repositories and fetch the package to be installed. Upon installation, we can use `tasksel` to install the LAMP server. To do this, we will have to invoke the `tasksel` program from the terminal by using the command `sudo tasksel`, as shown in the screenshot that follows:

```
File  Edit  View  Terminal  Go  Help
root@adminuser-1204-xbuntu:~#
root@adminuser-1204-xbuntu:~#
root@adminuser-1204-xbuntu:~#
root@adminuser-1204-xbuntu:~#
root@adminuser-1204-xbuntu:~#
root@adminuser-1204-xbuntu:~# sudo tasksel
```

 sudo is required to perform installation operations as normal users might not have the required privileges.

Upon invoking `tasksel` we will get a list of installable packages, such as the LAMP server, Tomcat server, and DNS server; we will be choosing the LAMP server. To navigate within the `tasksel` shell, we will use our arrows keys to move up and down, and the Space bar to select the program that has to be installed.

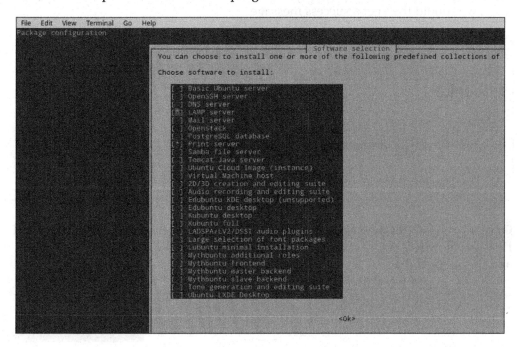

After selecting **LAMP server**, go ahead and press *Enter* to confirm the installation. Once the installation is complete, we are all set to write our first server-side program to generate and host a live JSON feed. To do this, we will navigate to the document root folder, which will be the only folder available to Apache. The document root folder is a folder where the files pertaining to a website or a web application are placed. Only web servers such as Apache, Tomcat, IIS, and Nginx are given access to these folders as unverified and anonymous users could get access to these files via the website. The default document root folder for Apache in Linux is the `/var/www` folder. To navigate to `/var/www`, we will use the `cd` command, which refers to change directory.

```
File    Edit    View    Terminal    Go    Help
root@adminuser-1204-xbuntu:~#
root@adminuser-1204-xbuntu:~#
root@adminuser-1204-xbuntu:~#
root@adminuser-1204-xbuntu:~#
root@adminuser-1204-xbuntu:~# cd /var/www/
```

Once we are in the www folder, we can start creating our server-side scripts. Apache already provides us with a test HTML page (in that folder) to test if Apache is up and running; it is named as the index.html. To perform this activity, we should open up a browser in the Linux operating system and access http://localhost/index. html; we should then get a success message.

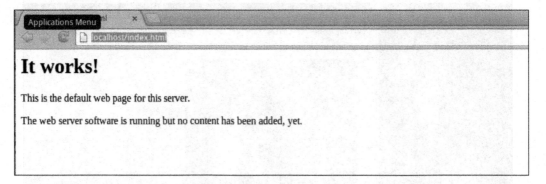

Once we receive this message we are assured that our Apache web server is up and running. Now let's set up a similar architecture using a Windows operating system and C# or ASP.NET.

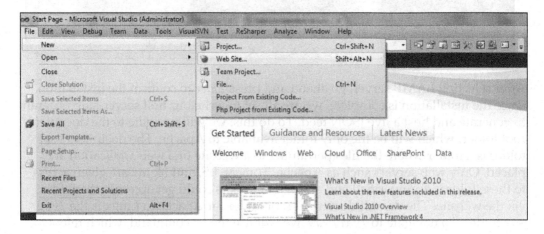

Microsoft Visual Studio is the chosen environment to develop server-side programs or web applications using ASP.NET and C#. Navigate to **File | New | Web Site**. Visual Studio comes along with its own development server for running a website during development.

Once we click on the **New Web Site** option, we will have to choose what type of a website we are building; since this is just a dummy website, let us keep it simple by choosing **ASP.NET Web Site** and then clicking on **OK**. This is shown in the preceding screenshot.

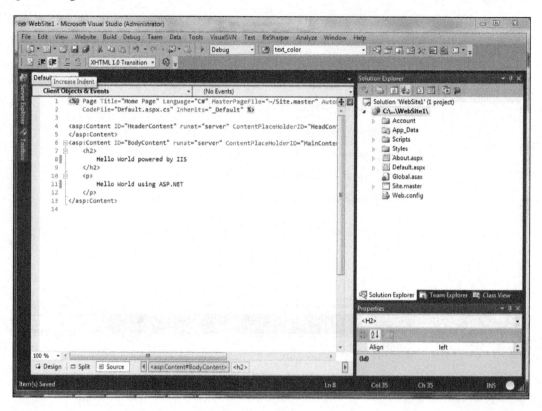

The default ASP.NET website comes with some basic HTML that can be used for testing; go ahead and click on the green button beside **Debug**. This is used to run the website; keep in mind that C# or ASP.NET programs have to be compiled before they can be run, unlike PHP or Python, which are interpreted languages.

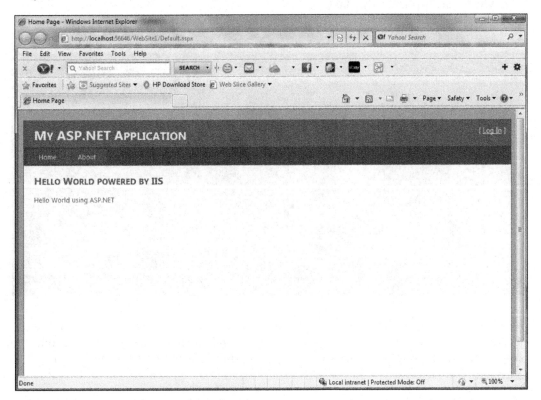

And here is our Hello World website application that is powered by C#/ASP.NET. Web applications can be built in any language, and JSON can be used as the data interchange language between web applications powered by any server-side stack. Let's take this knowledge of server-side programming and move forward on our journey so that we can implement this in powerful web applications.

Hosting JSON

In this section, we will be creating a PHP script that will allow us to send a JSON feedback to the user upon a successful request. Let's take a look at the index.php file, which accomplishes this task:

```php
<?php

    $students = array(
        array(
            "studentid" => "101",
            "firstname" => "John",
            "lastname"  => "Doe",
            "classes"   => array("Business Research", "Economics", "Finance")
        ),
        array(
            "studentid" => "101",
            "firstname" => "Jane",
            "lastname"  => "Dane",
            "classes"   => array("Marketing", "Economics", "Finance")
        )
    );

    header('Content-Type: application/json');
    echo json_encode($students);

?>
```

In this PHP script, we have created a basic students array and are generating the JSON feed for that array. The students array contains basic student information, such as the first name, last name, student ID, and the classes that the student has enrolled.

This file has to be placed in the www folder, and it should be on the same level as the default index.html file that comes with the LAMP installation. Refer to the folder structure in the following screenshot:

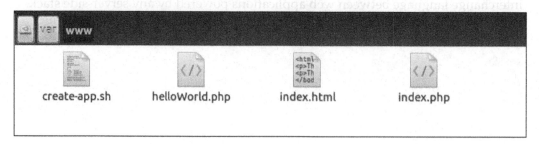

Now that our `index.php` is in the document root folder, we can load this file using our web server. To access this file via our Apache web server, navigate to `http://localhost/index.php`.

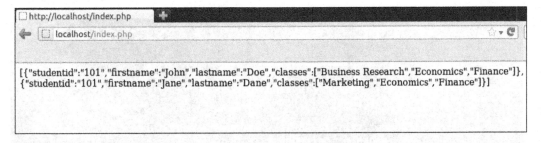

As shown in the preceding screenshot, when the file is run using the Apache web server, the server takes the request, parses the PHP code, and outputs the JSON feed that delivers the student data.

Making your first AJAX call

Now that we have an active JSON data feed, it is about time to make our first AJAX call. We will look at two approaches of making an AJAX call; these approaches come from different periods in time. The first approach will use basic JavaScript so that we understand what happens behind the scenes when an AJAX call is made. Once we understand the concept of AJAX, we will use a popular JavaScript library to make the same AJAX call but with simpler code. Let's take a look at our first approach using basic JavaScript:

```html
<!DOCTYPE html>
<html>
        <head>
                <title>First AJAX Script</title>
                <script type="text/javascript" src="index.js"></script>
        </head>
        <body>
                <h2>Include External JavaScript to make an AJAX call</h2>
                <p>This is a text program to make our
                        first AJAX call using JavaScript.</p>
        </body>
</html>
```

We will begin with our basic `index.html` file that loads an external JavaScript file. This JavaScript file performs the AJAX call to fetch the `students` JSON feed.

Let us take a look at `index.js`:

```
index.js                index.html          x
1
2   var request = new XMLHttpRequest();
3
4   request.open('GET', 'http://localhost/index.php');
5   request.onreadystatechange = function(){
6
7           if((request.status==200) && (request.readyState==4)){
8                   console.log(request.responseText);
9           }
10  }
11
12  request.send();
13
```

This is the original way in which an AJAX call is made to a live web server; let's break this script into pieces and investigate it piece by piece:

```
index.js          untitled          index.html       x
1
2   var request = new XMLHttpRequest();
3
```

In the preceding snippet we are creating an instance of the `XMLHttpRequest` object. The `XMLHttpRequest` object lets us make asynchronous calls to the server, thus allowing us to treat sections in the page as separate components. It comes with powerful properties such as `readystate`, `response`, `responseText`, and methods such as `open`, `onuploadprogress`, `onreadystatechange`, and `send`. Let's look at how we can use the `request` object that we have created to open an AJAX request:

```
index.js          untitled          index.html       x
1
2   request.open('GET', 'http://localhost/index.php');
3
```

`XMLHttpRequest`, by default, opens up an asynchronous request; here we will specify the method in which the live feed has to be contacted. As we will not be passing any data, we choose the HTTP `GET` method to send the data over to our live web server. While working on an asynchronous request, we should never have a blocking script; we can deal with this by setting up callbacks. A **callback** is a set of scripts that will be waiting for a response and will be fired on receiving that response. This behavior facilitates non-blocking code.

We are setting up a callback and are assigning the callback to a method called `onreadystatechange`, as shown in the following screenshot:

```
index.js          untitled          index.html          x
1
2    request.onreadystatechange = function(){
3
4            if((request.status==200) && (request.readyState==4)){
5                    console.log(request.responseText);
6            }
7    }
8
```

The placeholder method, `onreadystatechange`, looks for a property in the request object called `readyState`; whenever the value of `readyState` changes, the `onreadystatechange` event is fired. The `readyState` property keeps track of the progress of the `XMLHttpRequest` that is made. In the preceding screenshot, we can see the callback has a conditional statement that is verifying that the value of `readyState` is 4, meaning that the server has received the `XMLHttpRequest` that was made by the client and a response is ready. Let's take a quick look at the available values for `readyState`:

readyState	Description
0	The request hasn't been initialized
1	Server connection established
2	The server has received the request
3	The server is processing the request
4	The request has been processed and the response is ready

In the earlier screenshot, we are also looking for another property called the status; this is the HTTP status code that is coming back from the server. Status code 200 represents a successful transaction, while status code 400 is a bad request and 404 means Page Not Found. Other common status codes are 401, which means the user has requested a page that is available only for authorized users, and 500, which is an Internal Server Error.

We have created the XMLHttpRequest object and opened the connection; we have also added a callback to perform an event when the request is successful. One thing to keep in mind is that the request hasn't yet been made; we are only laying the foundation work for the request. We will use the send() method to send the request over to the server, as shown:

In our onreadystateChange callback, we are logging the response that is sent by the web server to the console window. Let's take a quick look at what the response looks like:

One way to confirm that this is an AJAX request is by looking at the first request in the console, where an asynchronous call is made to the index.php file and the response comes back with an HTTP status code of 200 OK. Since the HTTP status value is 200, the execution of the callback will be successful and it will output the students JSON feed onto the console window.

With the advent of powerful JavaScript libraries such as jQuery, Scriptaculous, Dojo, and ExtJS, we have moved away from the archaic process of making an AJAX request. One thing to keep in mind is that, though we do not use this process, the libraries will still be using this process under the hood; so having an idea of how the XMLHttpRequest object works is very important. jQuery is a very popular JavaScript library; it has a growing community with a lot of developers. As the jQuery library is distributed under the MIT License, it allows users to utilize this library free of cost.

jQuery is a very simple, powerful library with fantastic documentation and a strong user community that makes a developer's life very easy. Let's take a quick detour and write our customary Hello World program in jQuery:

```
index-jquery.html    x
1  <!DOCTYPE html>
2  <html>
3      <head>
4          <title>Hello World using JQuery</title>
5          <script type="text/javascript"
6              src="//ajax.googleapis.com/ajax/libs/jquery/1.10.2/jquery.min.js"></script>
7          <script>
8              $(document).ready(function(){
9                  console.log("Hello World!");
10             });
11         </script>
12     </head>
13     <body>
14         <h2>Hello World using JQuery</h2>
15         <p>This is a Hello World program using JQuery. </p>
16     </body>
17 </html>
18
```

In the preceding screenshot, we are importing the jQuery library into our HTML file, and in the second set of script tags, we are using the special character $ or jQuery. Similar to the concept of the namespace in object-oriented programming, the jQuery functionality is namespaced to the special character $ by default. jQuery has been a champion of unobtrusive JavaScript. After $, we call the document object and check whether the it has loaded onto the page; then we assign a callback function that will be triggered on a complete load of the document. "document" here the document object that holds the HTML element structure. The output for this program is going be the Hello World! string that will be outputted to our console window.

Parsing JSON data

Now that we are familiar with jQuery, let us trigger an AJAX request on an event such as a button click.

```
jquery-ajax.html        x    index.php        x
 1    <!DOCTYPE html>
 2    <html>
 3        <head>
 4            <title>AJAX using JQuery</title>
 5            <script type="text/javascript"
 6                src="//ajax.googleapis.com/ajax/libs/jquery/1.10.2/jquery.min.js"></script>
 7            <script>
 8                $(document).ready(function(){
 9                    $('#getFeed').click(function(){
10                        $.getJSON('/index.php', function(data){
11                            if(data){
12                                $.each(data, function(key, value){
13                                    $('#feedContainerList').append(
14                                    "<li>Student Id is "+ value.studentid+
15                                    " and the student name is "
16                                    + value.firstname+" "+ value.lastname+"</li>");
17                                });
18                            }
19                        });
20                    });
21                });
22            </script>
23        </head>
24        <body>
25            <h2>AJAX using JQuery</h2>
26            <input type="button" id="getFeed" value="Get Feed" />
27            <div id="feedContainer">
28                <ul id="feedContainerList">
29
30                </ul>
31            </div>
32        </body>
33    </html>
34
```

In this snippet, let us begin by observing the HTML document object. We have a div element that has an empty unordered list. The aim of this script is to populate the unordered list with list items on the click of a button. The input button element has an id with the value "getFeed", and the click event handler will be tied to this button. Since AJAX is asynchronous and as we are tying a callback to this button, no AJAX calls are made to our live server when the document object is loaded. The HTML structure alone is loaded onto the page, and the events are tied to these elements.

When the button is clicked on, we are using the method getJSON to make an AJAX call to the live web server to retrieve the JSON data. Since we are getting an array of students, we will pass the retrieved data into jQuerys' each iterator to retrieve one element at a time. Inside the iterator, we are building a string, which is appended as a list item to the "feedContainerList" unordered list element.

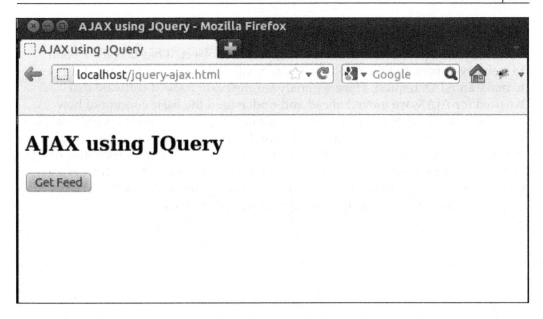

On loading of the document, as we are only binding our events to the HTML elements, there will not be any behavioral changes unless we click on the button. Once we click on the button, the unordered list will be populated.

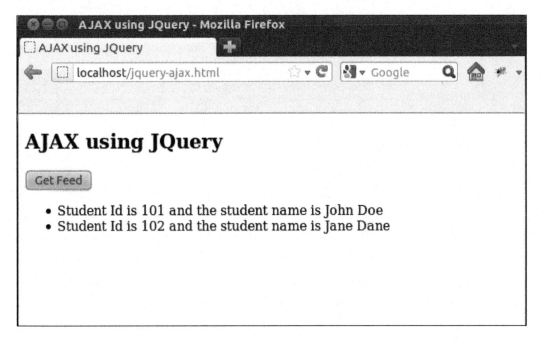

Summary

Since the rise in popularity of the XMLHttpRequest object, it has become a boon to web developers. In this chapter we began with the basics, such as what we need to make an AJAX request. Once we analyzed the basic stack of software that we need for AJAX, we moved ahead and understood the basic concept of how an XMLHttpRequest object is responsible for making an asynchronous request. Then we took a leap into one of the most powerful JavaScript Libraries, jQuery, to perform AJAX operations using jQuery. This is just the beginning of our journey into AJAX; in the next chapter we will be looking at more complex cases where AJAX is used, the cases where cross-domain asynchronous requests fail, and how JSON saves the day by allowing us to make cross-domain asynchronous calls.

5
Cross-domain Asynchronous Requests

In the previous chapter, we used jQuery's getJSON method to ingest the students JSON feed; in this chapter we will take a step forward and send request parameters over to the server. Data feeds are often large amounts of data that are made available; the data that is part of such feeds is normally generic and can be considered too heavy for a targeted search. For example, in the students JSON feed, we are exposing the whole list of student information that is available. For a data vendor who is looking for students who are enrolled in certain courses or who reside in a given ZIP code to hire them as interns, this feed is going to be generic. It is common to see development teams build **Application Programming Interfaces** or **APIs** to give such data vendors numerous ways to target their search. This is a win-win situation for both the data vendor and for the company that owns the information since the data vendor only gets the information that they are looking for and the data supplier only sends the requested data, thereby saving a lot of bandwidth and server resources.

Making GET and POST AJAX calls with JSON data

It is important to understand that both synchronous and asynchronous calls are made over HTTP, so the data transfer process is the same. The popular methods to transfer data from the client machine to the server machine are GET and POST. The most common request method in HTTP is GET. When a client requests a web page, the web server uses the URL to process the HTTP request. Any other parameters that are appended to the URL serve as the data that is being sent from the client to the server. Since the parameters are part of the URL, it is important to make a clear distinction between when to and when not to use the GET request method. The GET method should be used to pass idempotent information such as a page number, a link address, or the limits and offsets that are a part of pagination. Keep in mind that there is a size constraint as to how much data can be transferred via the GET request method.

The POST request method is commonly used while sending the data that is big in size and that is non-trivial. Unlike the GET method, the data is transferred through the HTTP message body; we can use tools such as Fiddler and the developer tools available in the browser to track the data that is going out through the HTTP message body. The data that is being passed through the POST method cannot be bookmarked or cached, unlike the GET method. The POST method is often used to send data while using forms. For our examples in this chapter, let us use jQuery's ajax method to send data over to the server in JSON format. We will be working with a modified students API where we will be able to query complete student information—the ZIP code they live in, the classes that they take, and so on—and use a combination search to find students who live in a certain area and are taking a certain class. A new addition to our API is the functionality to add a student via a POST request; the student information has to be sent as a JSON object.

 This API is built in PHP and MySQL. The PHP and MySQL files would be made available in the scripts-chap5 folder present in the code bundle..

Before we start building scripts to make our asynchronous calls, let's take a look at the URLs that our `students` API provides. The first API call will be the generic search that will retrieve information for all the students in the database.

```
untitled
1
2    http://www.training.com/getStudents.php
3
```

As we have not started our targeted search, the URL has been kept for a generic search. Now let's look at the URL for our first targeted search—by ZIP code. This API call will return all the students that reside in the given ZIP code area.

```
untitled
1
2    http://www.training.com/getStudents.php?zip_code=08810
3    |
```

In this example, the URL will return the information for all the students that reside in the ZIP code 08810. Let's switch the search criteria from the ZIP code to the class that a student has enrolled into.

```
untitled
1
2    http://www.training.com/getStudents.php?class=Economics
3
```

In this example, the URL will return information for all the students that have enrolled for the class `Economics`. Now that we have the power of targeting the search by a ZIP code and a class, let us look at another call in our API to retrieve information by using both the ZIP code that the user resides in and the class that he or she has enrolled in.

```
untitled
1
2    http://www.training.com/getStudents.php?class=Accounting&zip_code=77082
3
```

In this example, a call to the URL will return information for all the students that have enrolled for the class `Accounting` and reside in the ZIP code 77082.

The calls had until now used the HTTP GET method to transfer data from the client to the server. The last call in our API is powered by the HTTP POST method for adding a student. This call needs heavy data input, as a user can have multiple ZIP codes and multiple addresses and can be enrolled in multiple classes.

```
untitled
1
2  http://www.training.com/addUser.php
3
```

As this is an HTTP POST method, none of the data that is being passed in is visible. Let's move forward with our scripts to access these calls; the first script will be to access the API call that provides information for all the students.

The following is the code snippet for get-students.html:

```
get-students.html    x
1  <!DOCTYPE html>
2  <html>
3      <head>
4          <title>Get all students</title>
5          <script type="text/javascript"
6              src="//ajax.googleapis.com/ajax/libs/jquery/1.10.2/jquery.min.js"></script>
7          <script>
8              $(document).ready(function(){
9                  $.ajax({
10                     "url":"/getStudents.php",
11                     "type":"GET",
12                     "data":{},
13                     "dataType":"JSON"
14                 }).done(function(data){
15                     console.log(data);
16                 });
17             });
18         </script>
19     </head>
20     <body>
21         <h2>Get all students</h2>
22         <p>Retrieve the students information of all students</p>
23     </body>
24 </html>
25
```

In this call we start by importing the jQuery library; we can start using the $ variable as we have jQuery on the page. We begin by adding a callback that is fired when the document is ready. We are using the ajax method for this example as it allows us to make the GET and POST requests, and when required, we can modify the datatype property in the ajax call to JSONP to make asynchronous cross-domain calls.

It is not necessary to explicitly mention when the type is GET, but it helps us build consistency with our code.

In our `ajax` call we begin by setting the `url` property to the link to our API call to retrieve the student information; we specify that this will be performed via the HTTP GET method. The fourth property that we are setting is the `dataType` property; this is used to mention the type of the data that we are expecting returned. As we are working with the `students` feed, we will have to set the `dataType` property to JSON. It is important to note the `done` callback that is fired when the server sends a response back to our asynchronous request. We are passing the data that is sent over from the server as a response, initiating the callback.

done is the same as `readyState=4` and `request.status=200`; we have looked at this in *Chapter 4, AJAX Calls with JSON Data*, while making asynchronous calls using JavaScript.

The following is the output:

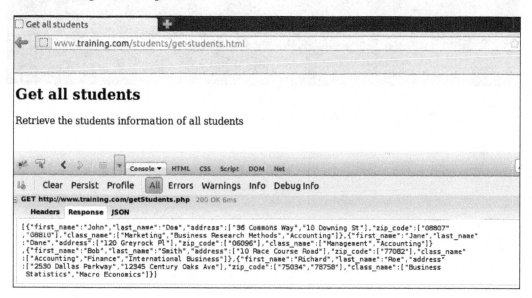

In the console window, we can view the JSON feed response that comes back from the server. This JSON feed contains a lot of information, as it gets the data for all the students. Now let us fetch the student records based on the ZIP code. For this example, we will be using the `zip_code` parameter and will asynchronously pass a value to the server via the HTTP GET method. This API call will serve the purpose for data vendors who want to search for interns who are available in a specific area.

```
targeted-student-search-zip.html ×
1  <!DOCTYPE html>
2  <html>
3      <head>
4          <title>Targeted Student Search</title>
5          <script type="text/javascript"
6              src="//ajax.googleapis.com/ajax/libs/jquery/1.10.2/jquery.min.js"></script>
7          <script>
8              $(document).ready(function(){
9                  $.ajax({
10                     "url":"/getStudents.php",
11                     "type":"GET",
12                     "data":{"zip_code":"08810"},
13                     "dataType":"JSON"
14                 }).done(function(data){
15                     console.log(data);
16                 });
17             });
18         </script>
19     </head>
20     <body>
21         <h2>Targeted Student Search</h2>
22         <p>Retrieving student information based on the zip code.</p>
23     </body>
24  </html>
25
```

In the previous example, we start by importing the jQuery library and we bind a callback to ready the event that is fired when the document has loaded. It is important to notice that we are sending a key-value pair for the ZIP code using the data property in line 12.

Once the call is fired, we log the response to the console window. The ZIP code 08810 matches one user, and the student information is being passed back via the JSON feed. Targeted searches help us narrow down our results, thereby providing us with the data that we are looking for; the next target search in line would be to retrieve data using a certain class that a student is enrolled in.

```html
1  <!DOCTYPE html>
2  <html>
3      <head>
4          <title>Targeted Student Search</title>
5          <script type="text/javascript"
6              src="//ajax.googleapis.com/ajax/libs/jquery/1.10.2/jquery.min.js"></script>
7          <script>
8              $(document).ready(function(){
9                  $.ajax({
10                     "url":"/getStudents.php",
11                     "type":"GET",
12                     "data":{"class":"Economics"},
13                     "dataType":"JSON"
14                 }).done(function(data){
15                     console.log(data);
16                 });
17             });
18         </script>
19     </head>
20     <body>
21         <h2>Targeted Student Search</h2>
22         <p>Retrieving student information based on classes they are enrolled in.</p>
23     </body>
24 </html>
25
```

The previous example is the same as the targeted search with ZIP code; here we are replacing the ZIP code information with the class information. We are retrieving all the students who have enrolled for `Economics`.

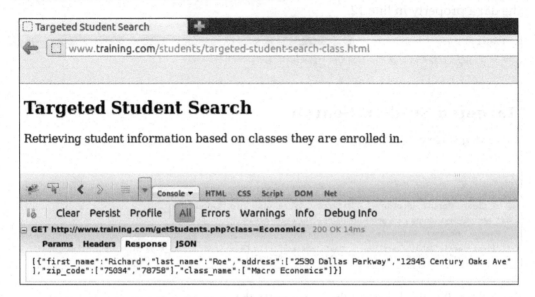

The targeted search returns student information for those who have enrolled for an Economics class. Now let us target our search with a combination of class and ZIP code.

```
targeted-student-search-class-zip.html  ×
1   <!DOCTYPE html>
2   <html>
3       <head>
4           <title>Targeted Student Search</title>
5           <script type="text/javascript"
6               src="//ajax.googleapis.com/ajax/libs/jquery/1.10.2/jquery.min.js"></script>
7           <script>
8               $(document).ready(function(){
9                   $.ajax({
10                      "url":"/getStudents.php",
11                      "type":"GET",
12                      "data":{"class":"Accounting", "zip_code":"77082"},
13                      "dataType":"JSON"
14                  }).done(function(data){
15                      console.log(data);
16                  });
17              });
18          </script>
19      </head>
20      <body>
21          <h2>Targeted Student Search</h2>
22          <p>Retrieving student information based on classes they are enrolled in
23              and the zip code.</p>
24
25      </body>
26  </html>
27
```

In the previous example, we add the class and the ZIP code key-value pairs to send multiple search parameters to the server.

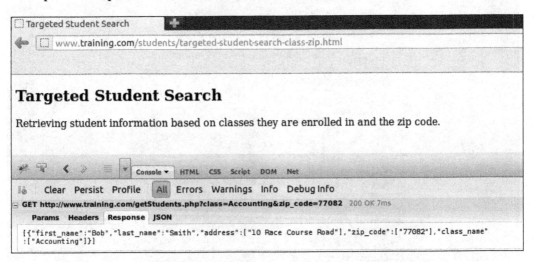

This call retrieves the student information for students who have enrolled for the `Accounting` course and reside in the ZIP code `77082`. We have seen multiple examples of making asynchronous calls via the HTTP `GET` method; now it is time for us to push the data onto the server in order to add a student using our API. We will be using our `addUser` call to add a student on the fly. This helps the development teams to add student information into our database from external resources. For example, we are a student information aggregator and we sell consolidated student information to multiple data vendors. For us to aggregate all this information, we might be aggregating it via spiders, where a script would go to a website and fetch the data, or external resources, where the data will be unstructured. So we will structure our data and use this `addUser` API call to ingest the structured student data information into our data storage. Simultaneously, we can expose this method to trusted data vendors who would like to store the student information that is not available with us, thereby helping them to make our data storage a single point data location. It is a win-win for both the companies as we get more student information and our data vendors get to store their student information on a remote location. Now let's take a look at how this `addUser` post call will be made.

```
7     <script>
8         $(document).ready(function(){
9
10            var first_name = "Kent";
11            var last_name = "Clark";
12
13            var addresses = ["5400 W Parmer Ln", "1919 Elridge Pkwy"];
14            var zip_codes = ["78757", "77087"];
15            var classes = ["International Business", "Economics Statistics"];
16
17            $.ajax({
18                "url":"addUser.php",
19                "type":"POST",
20                "data":{
21                    "first_name":first_name,
22                    "last_name":last_name,
23                    "addresses":addresses,
24                    "zip_codes":zip_codes,
25                    "classes":classes
26                },
27                "content-type":"application/json; charset=utf-8",
28                "dataType":"JSON"
29            }).done(function(data){
30                console.log(data);
31            });
32        });
33     </script>
```

In this call, we are doing multiple things; we start by declaring a few variables to hold local data. We have local variables that hold string values for the first name and last name of the student, and we also have variables that are holding arrays for classes, ZIP codes, and addresses, as Superman has to be at multiple locations in a span of few minutes. In our `ajax` call, the first change to note is the `type` property; as we are pushing a large amount of user data, it is common to use the HTTP POST method. The `data` property is going to use the local variables that are declared for the first name, last name, addresses, ZIP codes, and the classes. From the API, when a user is added to the database successfully, we send a success message in response, and that will be logged to our console window.

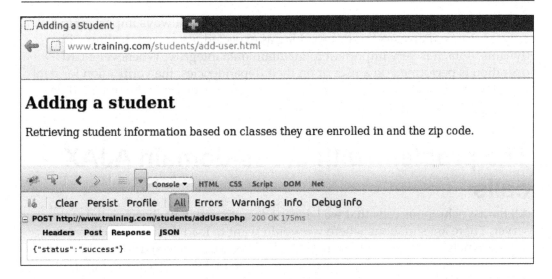

Now to verify that the new student has been added to our database, we can run our getStudents API call to see a list of all the users.

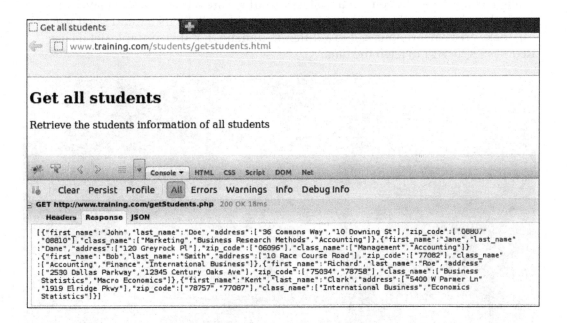

The last student in the `students` feed is `Kent Clark`; it is always important to test our code to see that everything is working as expected. As we are dealing with dynamic data, it is very important to maintain data integrity. Whenever a CRUD operation is performed on a user or on their dependencies, the verification for data integrity on that data storage has to be performed by looking at the retrieved data and by performing data validation checks.

The problem with cross-domain AJAX calls

All the asynchronous calls that we have made until now have been on the same server. There are situations where we would want to load data from a different domain, such as fetching data from other APIs. Server-side programs are designed to handle these kinds of calls; we can use cURL to make HTTP calls to different domains to fetch such data. This increases our dependency on server-side programs as we would have to make a call to our server, which would in turn make a call to another domain to fetch the data, which would be returned to a client-side program. It might come across as being a trivial issue, but we are adding an extra layer to our web architecture. To avoid making a server-side call, let us try and see if we can make an asynchronous call to a different domain. For this example, let us use Reddit's JSON API to fetch the data.

```html
<!DOCTYPE html>
<html>
    <head>
        <title>Asynchronous Call to Reddit</title>
        <script type="text/javascript"
            src="//ajax.googleapis.com/ajax/libs/jquery/1.10.2/jquery.min.js"></script>
        <script>
            $(document).ready(function(){
                $.ajax({
                    "url":"http://www.reddit.com/.json",
                    "type":"GET",
                    "data":{},
                    "dataType":"JSON"
                }).done(function(data){
                    console.log(data);
                });
            });
        </script>
    </head>
    <body>
        <h2>Asynchronous Call to Reddit</h2>
        <p>Asynchronous call to the website reddit.com</p>
    </body>
</html>
```

This is similar to the asynchronous calls that we have made earlier to retrieve data from our `students` API. It is important to understand that we did not have to mention the whole URL in the previous cases as we were making a call to the same domain.

The Reddit site provides an excellent JSON API, whereby we can append `.json` to the URL and will get the JSON feed for that aggregated web page, given that the page is part of Reddit. Let's take a look at the output that is generated when we make this asynchronous call across domains.

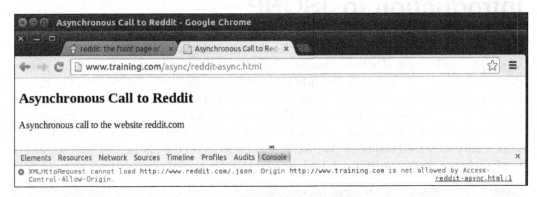

In our asynchronous call, the data would have been logged to the console window, if the request were successful, but we see an error in the console window. The error says that the `XMLHTTPRequest` object cannot load the URL that we have provided as it doesn't originate from our `www.training.com` domain. The **same domain policy** is a security measure followed by web browsers in order to prevent one domain from accessing information on another domain. Web applications use cookies to store basic information about a user's session so as to provide an intuitive user experience when the user requests the same web page another time or requests a different web page on the same domain. To prevent an external website from stealing this information, web browsers follow the **same origin policy**.

The same domain policy looks for three things in an incoming request; they are the host, the port, and the protocol. If any of them is different from the existing domain, the request will not be completed and the cross-domain error is returned.

Variant of http://www.training.com	RESULT
`http://www.training.com/index.php`	PASS
`https://www.training.com/index.php`	FAIL (Protocol)
`http://www.training:81.com/index.php`	FAIL (Port)
`http://test.training.com.com/index.php`	FAIL (Host)
`http://www.differentsite.com/index.php`	FAIL (Host)

Introduction to JSONP

In order to get around the same origin policy, we will be using JSONP, which is JSON with Padding. One exception under the same origin policy is the `<script>` tag so scripts can be passed across domains. JSONP uses this exception in order to pass data across domains as a script by adding padding to make the JSON object look like a script. In JavaScript, when a function with a parameter is invoked, we call the function and add a parameter. With JSONP, we pass the JSON feed as a parameter to a function; thereby, we pad our object into a function callback. This function into which the JSON feed has been padded has to be used on the client-side to retrieve the JSON feed. Let's take a quick look at a JSONP example.

```
untitled
1
2   myCallback({
3       "studentid": "101",
4       "firstname": "John",
5       "lastname": "Doe",
6       "classes": [
7           "Business Research",
8           "Economics",
9           "Finance"
10       ]
11   });
12
```

In this example, we are padding the `students` object into the `myCallback` function and we have to reuse the `myCallback` function in order to retrieve the `students` object. Now that we understand how JSONP works, let's use Reddit's JSON API to fetch the data. We need to make one change to the way we access the data—we need to find a way to pad the feed into a callback that can be used on the client-side. The Reddit website provide a `jsonp` GET parameter that will take the name of the callback to provide the data.

getRedditData({"kind": "Listing", "data": {"modhash": "", "children": [{"kind": "t3", "data": {"domain": "deathandtaxesmag.com", "banned_by": null, "media_embed": {}, "subreddit": "science", "selftext_html": null, "selftext": "", "likes": null, "secure_media": null, "saved": false, "id": "1mgcny", "secure_media_embed": {}, "clicked": false, "stickied": false, "author": "seanl2012", "media": null, "score": 1, "approved_by": null, "over_18": false, "hidden": false, "thumbnail": "", "subreddit_id": "t5_mouw", "edited": false, "link_flair_css_class": null, "author_flair_css_class": null, "downs": 0, "is_self": false, "permalink": "/r/science/comments/1mgcny/nigerian_student_uses_magnets_to_prove_gay/", "name": "t3_1mgcny", "created": 1379307408.0, "url": "http://www.deathandtaxesmag.com/205755/nigerian-student-uses-magnets-to-prove-gay-marriage-scientifically-impossible/", "author_flair_text": null, "title": "Nigerian student uses magnets to prove gay marriage scientifically impossible", "created_utc": 1379278608.0, "link_flair_text": null, "ups": 1, "num_comments": 0, "num_reports": null, "distinguished": null}}, {"kind": "t3", "data": {"domain": "youtube.com", "banned_by": null, "media_embed": {}, "subreddit": "Music", "selftext_html": null, "selftext": "", "likes": null, "secure_media": null, "saved": false, "id": "1mgcnt", "secure_media_embed": {}, "clicked": false, "stickied": false, "author": "Mac3030", "media": null, "score": 1, "approved_by": null, "over_18": false, "hidden": false, "thumbnail": "",

Implementing JSONP

We are using the same URL as before to fetch the data, but we have added the jsonp parameter and are setting it to getRedditData; it is important to note that the feed is now padded into our callback getRedditData. Now let's replace the URL property in our earlier script to create a new script that will fetch us the JSON feed.

```html
<!DOCTYPE html>
<html>
    <head>
        <title>JSONP Call to Reddit</title>
        <script type="text/javascript"
            src="//ajax.googleapis.com/ajax/libs/jquery/1.10.2/jquery.min.js"></script>
        <script>
            $(document).ready(function(){
                $.ajax({
                    "url":"http://www.reddit.com/.json?jsonp=getRedditData",
                    "type":"GET",
                    "dataType":"jsonp",
                    "contentType": "application/json",
                    "jsonpCallback":"getRedditData",
                    "success":function(data){
                        console.log(data);
                    }
                })
            });
        </script>
    </head>
    <body>
        <h2>JSONP Call to Reddit</h2>
        <p>JSONP call to the website reddit.com</p>
    </body>
</html>
```

A few properties such as `url` and `dataType` have been modified and a few new properties such as `contentType` and `jsonpCallback` have been added. We have already discussed the change in the `url` property, so let us look at the other properties.

```
"dataType":"jsonp",
"contentType": "application/json",
"jsonpCallback":"getRedditData",
```

Earlier, the `dataType` property was set to `json` as the incoming feed was of type `json`, but now the JSON feed is being padded into a callback, and it has to be switched so that the browser expects a callback rather than JSON itself. The new properties that have been added are `contentType` and `jsonpCallback`; the property `contentType` specifies the type of content being sent to the web server. `jsonpCallback` takes the name of the callback function into which the JSON feed has been padded.

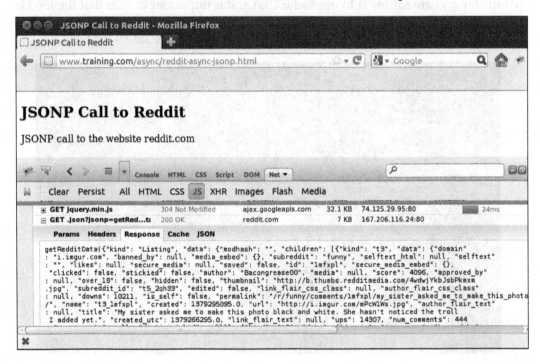

When the script is fired, the data from the `getRedditData` callback has been retrieved and is passed over into the `success` property that logs our JSON object onto the console window. An important fact to make a note of is that a JSONP call is a script call and not an XHR request, so the JSONP call will be available in the `JS` or `<scripts>` tab and not in the `XHR` tab of the console window.

Summary

HTTP `GET` and `POST` request methods are two of the most popular HTTP methods that are used to transfer data from clients to servers. This chapter provides an in-depth understanding of how `GET` and `POST` request methods are used to transfer data using asynchronous requests. We then proceeded to look at what the issues are with cross-domain asynchronous requests; we used the exception of the `<script>` tag to perform our JSONP asynchronous script calls to fetch the data from a different domain. In the next chapter, we will be building our photo gallery application.

6
Building the Carousel Application

We have come a long way in our journey to master JavaScript and JSON; it is time to get busy and build an end-to-end project that is powered by JSON. In our journey, we have come across a variety of concepts such as JavaScript, JSON, the use of server-side programming, AJAX, and JSONP. In this photo gallery application, let us put all of these to use. We will be building a rotating notification board application, which should display the top students for the month. This application should provide the Carousel functionality, such as navigational buttons, auto play of content, displaying a single item at a given point, and keeping track of the first and last piece of content.

Setting up the application

Let us begin by building a folder that will hold the files for this application. This application will need an HTML file that will hold the Carousel; it will need a few libraries such as jQuery and jQuery Cycle. We will have to import these libraries; we also need a JSON file that holds the data for this exercise. To download the jQuery file, please visit `http://www.jquery.com`. As we have already observed, jQuery is the most popular JavaScript library available to developers. There is a growing community of developers who make jQuery more and more popular by the day. We will be using the jQuery Cycle library to power our Carousel application. The jQuery Cycle is one the most popular and lightweight cycle libraries with numerous features; it can be downloaded from `http://malsup.github.io/jquery.cycle.all.js`.

These files have to be in a folder inside your document root; in this project we will be working with a live Apache Server, and we will be ingesting the JSON feed via AJAX. The following is an example of how the folder should look once the files have been added:

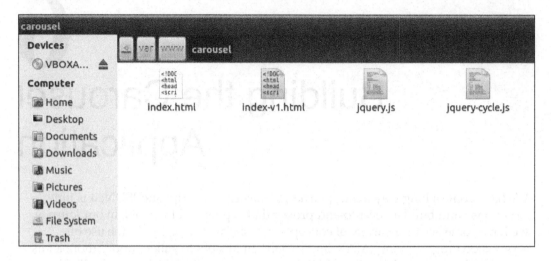

Now that we have the libraries arranged in the document root, let us work on the basic HTML file that will import these files into the web page, as shown in the following screenshot:

```
1   <!DOCTYPE html>
2   <html>
3       <head>
4           <!--Importing JQuery Library-->
5           <script type="text/javascript" src="jquery.js"></script>
6           <!--Importing JQuery Cycle Library-->
7           <script type="text/javascript" src="jquery-cycle.js"></script>
8           <!--Local JavaScript for DOM Manipulation-->
9           <script type="text/javascript">
10              $(document).ready(function(){
11                  console.log('ready');
12              });
13          </script>
14      </head>
15      <body>
16
17      </body>
18  </html>
19
```

index-v1.html

This is our initial index web page that will load the JavaScript files onto the web page. When this file is fired up via a web browser, both the JavaScript libraries have to be loaded and `ready` should be printed onto the console window. Now, let's move forward and build our Carousel application. Next in the line of requirements is the data file; it will be similar to the `students` JSON feed that we have worked with in our previous chapters. Rather than printing them all in a single line, we will be loading them into a rotator application.

Building the JSON file for the Carousel application

Let us assume that we are an educational institution, and we have a tradition of acknowledging the efforts of our students on a monthly basis. We will pick the top students from each course for that month, and display their names on our notice board rotator application. This notice board rotator application has often served as a motivation for other students, who always aim to get themselves onto that board. This is the way our educational institution is encouraging the students to do well in their courses. The example JSON feed will look like the following screenshot:

```json
{
    "studentid": "101",
    "firstname": "John",
    "lastname": "Doe",
    "level": "Freshman",
    "class": "Environmental Toxicology"
},
```

For our notice board rotator application, we will need basic student information, such as the first name, last name, current level of education, and the course that they have excelled in.

```html
students.json          x    index-v2.html          x
1    <!DOCTYPE html>
2    <html>
3        <head>
4            <!--Importing JQuery Library-->
5            <script type="text/javascript" src="jquery.js"></script>
6            <!--Importing JQuery Cycle Library-->
7            <script type="text/javascript" src="jquery-cycle.js"></script>
8            <!--Local JavaScript for DOM Manipulation-->
9            <script type="text/javascript">
10               $(document).ready(function(){
11                   $.getJSON('students.json',function(data){
12                       console.log(data);
13                   });
14               });
15           </script>
16       </head>
17       <body>
18
19       </body>
20   </html>
21
```

index-v2.html

In the preceding screenshot, we are using jQuery's getJSON() function to bring the JSON feed into the document. When the index-v2.html file is loaded into the browser, the students JSON object array will be loaded onto the console window. It is about time to start extracting data from the JSON object, and to start embedding them onto the DOM. Let's use the jQuery each() function to loop over the students JSON feed and load the data onto the page.

The each() function in jQuery is similar to the foreach() iterative loop, which is available with the popular server-side languages, and the for in() iterative loop, which is available in the native JavaScript. The each() iterator takes the data as its first argument, and passes the each item in that data iteratively as a single key-value pair into a callback. This callback is a collection of a number of scripts that are executed on that key-value pair. In this callback, we are building the HTML file that will be appended to a div element on the DOM. We are using this callback to iteratively build the HTML file for all the elements that exist in that students JSON object.

```
1  <!DOCTYPE html>
2  <html>
3      <head>
4          <!-- Importing JQuery Library -->
5          <script type="text/javascript" src="jquery.js"></script>
6          <!-- Importing JQuery Cycle Library -->
7          <script type="text/javascript" src="jquery-cycle.js"></script>
8          <!-- Local JavaScript for DOM Manipulation -->
9          <script type="text/javascript">
10             var html = '';
11             $(document).ready(function(){
12                 $.getJSON('students.json',function(data){
13
14                     $.each(data, function(key, value){
15
16                         $.each(value, function(index, student){
17                             html += '<div class="student">';
18
19                             html += '<h2>'+ student.level+' of the Month</h3>';
20
21                             html += '<h4>'+student.firstname+
22                                 ' '+ student.lastname+'</h4>';
23
24                             html += '<p>'+ student.class+'</p>';
25
26                             html += '</div>';
27                         })
28                     });
29
30                     $('#students').html(html);
31                 });
32             });
33         </script>
```

index-v3.html

In the `index-v3.html` file, we are using the jQuery `each()` function to iterate through the `students` JSON feed, and build the HTML file that will display the student information, such as the first name, last name, the year of college, and the course that they are enrolled in. We are building the dynamic HTML and assigning it to the `html` variable. The data in the `html` variable will be added later to the `div` element with an ID of `students`. This is shown in the following screenshot:

```
1
2  <body>
3
4      <div id="students"></div>
5
6  </body>
7
```

The proceeding screenshot shows the output of the index-v3.html body:

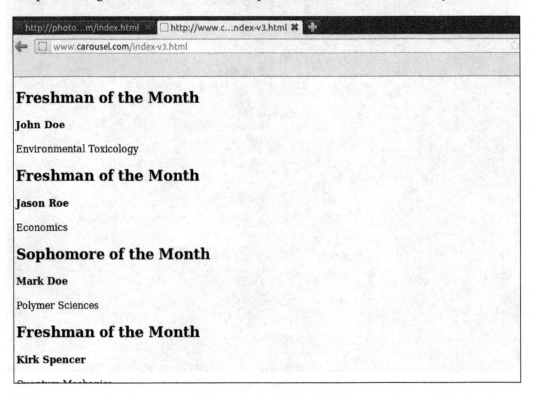

When the script is loaded into a web browser, the script checks to see if the document is ready. Once the document is ready, an AJAX call is made to the server to retrieve the JSON data. Once the JSON data is retrieved, each object in the students JSON object array feed will be passed into the callback that generates an HTML div element with a class student. This repeats until the callback is run on the last element, and once the callback is executed on the last element, this HTML file will be appended to a div element in the HTML with an ID of students.

Creating the Carousel application with jQuery Cycle

We have developed a web page that loads all the student data into an HTML file; now it is time to build the Carousel application using this data. We will be using a jQuery Cycle plugin to rotate the student information on our notice board application. The jQuery Cycle is a slideshow plugin that supports various types of transition effects on multiple browsers. Effects such as `fade`, `toss`, `wipe`, `zoom`, `scroll`, and `shuffle` are available. The plugin also supports the interesting pause on hover feature; click triggers and response callbacks are also supported.

For our Carousel example, let's keep it simple and use the basic options, such as a fade effect to rotate the students, enabling the pause so that whenever a user hovers onto the cycle, the rotator application is paused to display the information of the current student. Finally, we will be setting the speed and the timeout values that will determine how much time it will take to transition from one student to another.

```
students.json          index-v4.html          untitled

1
2    var html = '';
3 ▼  $(document).ready(function(){
4 ▼      $.getJSON('students.json',function(data){
5
6 ▼          $.each(data, function(key, value){
7
8 ▼              $.each(value, function(index, student){
9                   html += '<div class="student">';
10
11                  html += '<h2>'+ student.level+' of the Month</h3>';
12
13                  html += '<h4>'+student.firstname+
14                       ' '+ student.lastname+'</h4>';
15
16                  html += '<p>'+ student.class+'</p>';
17
18                  html += '</div>';
19              })
20          });
21
22          $('#students').html(html);
23
24 ▼        $('#students').cycle({
25              fx:'fade',
26              pause:'1',
27              speed:500,
28              timeout: 10000
29          });
30      });
31  });
32
```

index-v4.html

In the preceding screenshot, we set up the `cycle` plugin, and added the `cycle` plugin to the `div` element of `students`. The `cycle` plugin takes a JSON object as its parameter, to add the rotator functionality to a `div` element. In this JSON object we have added four properties: `fx`, `pause`, `speed`, and `timeout`. `fx` determines the effect that is performed on the `html` element. `fade` is a prominent effect that is used for the `cycle` plugin. The other popular effects that are supported by the jQuery Cycle plugin are shuffle, zoom, turndown, scrollRight, and curtainX. The second property we are using is the `pause` property, this determines whether the rotation has stopped when the user hovers onto the `rotator` element; it takes a true and false value to determine if the rotation can be paused or not. We could either supply a Boolean value such as True or False, or pass one or zero that signify True and False respectively. The next two properties are `speed` and `timeout`; they determine the speed with which the rotation occurs and how much time it will take before the next item is displayed. When the web page with the updated script is loaded into a web browser, the whole `students` object is parsed into a local JavaScript string variable and is appended to the DOM, and only the first element in that rotator object is displayed while the rest of them are hidden. This functionality is handled behind-the-scenes by the `cycle` plugin. The following screenshot displays a Carousel generated from the earlier code sample:

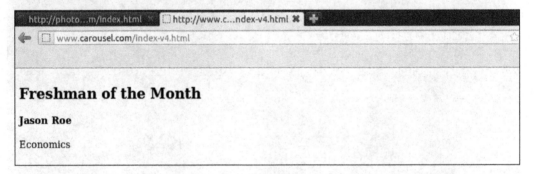

Let us enhance the user experience of this page by adding the earlier and following handlers to give the users custom controllers to handle the rotator functionality, as shown in the following screenshot:

```
var html = '';
$(document).ready(function(){
    $.getJSON('students.json',function(data){

        $.each(data, function(key, value){

            $.each(value, function(index, student){
                html += '<div class="student">';

                html += '<h2>'+ student.level+' of the Month</h3>';

                html += '<h4>'+student.firstname+
                    ' '+ student.lastname+'</h4>';

                html += '<p>'+ student.class+'</p>';

                html += '</div>';
            })
        });

        $('#students').html(html);

        $('#students').cycle({
            fx:'fade',
            pause:'1',
            prev:'#prev',
            next:'#next',
            speed:500,
            timeout: 10000
        });
    });
});
```

index-v5.html

In the `cycle` object, we are adding two new properties called `prev` and `next`. The values for the `prev` and `next` properties will be the HTML `id` attributes of elements that are on the DOM. The HTML file has to be modified as follows in order to handle this change:

```
    <body>
        <a href="#" id="prev">Prev</a>
        <a href="#" id="next">Next</a>
        <div id="students"></div>
    </body>
```

In the preceding screenshot, we have added two anchor element with `id` values of `prev` and `next` that are being referenced in the `cycle` object.

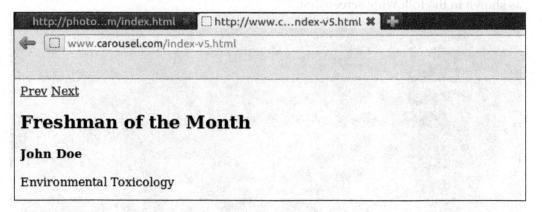

The **Prev** and **Next** links that are shown in the preceding screenshot are going to handle the rotation of our notice board rotation application. This is a quick way of building a Carousel application that is powered by jQuery and JSON. This example can used to build more complex Carousel applications that can contain images and videos for the photo and video gallery Carousel applications respectively.

Summary

In this chapter we put our JavaScript, jQuery, and JSON knowledge to work, and built up a neat little Carousel notice board rotator application. We went through a step-by-step process to ingest the data feed, build a dynamic template on the fly from that data feed, append the data feed to a `div` element, and then bind the `div` element to the `cycle` plugin. This notice board rotator application gives us an insight to bigger Carousel projects that can be developed with very little development effort. In the next chapter, we will look at the alternative implementations of JSON.

Alternate Implementations of JSON

In the chapters until now, we have worked with JSON as an HTTP data interchange format; now let's look at the popular alternate methods in which JSON is being used. In the last few years, there has been a sharp rise in the number of software modules and packages across all programming and scripting languages. Crowdsourcing software development has been on an upward climb. Web-based hosting services such as SourceForge, Pastebin, and GitHub have gained popularity in the last few years, and they have opened up doors for developers to collaborate and contribute back to the community. These modules and packages can be independently integrated or can be used as dependent programs with an existing software framework. This behavior has been a common practice in the open source community where developers can work independently to contribute software packages that enhance the frameworks that they are working with.

Scripting languages such as PHP, Python, and JavaScript have a huge number of contributed software packages and modules. The advantage here is to use a prebuilt software package that provides certain functionality out of the box and has been heavily tested by the community. The flip side of introducing a single framework or multiple frameworks into a software project is having to understand how these frameworks are loaded into the project, how they can be accessed from different sections in the current project, whether these frameworks have any dependencies, and finally, how they affect the whole project. These issues can be addressed by using a **dependency manager**.

A dependency manager is a software program that keeps track of all the necessary base programs that are required for a dependent program to run. A common practice in a software development life cycle is to perform unit tests by using a unit-testing framework; the unit-testing framework in turn might need some base libraries to be installed or there might be a few settings to enable the use of that framework.

These operations are often handled by writing up quick scripts, but as the project grows bigger, the dependencies grow along with the project. Along the same lines, tracking these changes and making sure different teams working on the project get these updates, which is done by scripts, is a tough task. By introducing a dependency manager, we will be automating the whole process, which adds consistency and saves time.

Dependency management

Dependency management has often been a little rocky, and for new developers who are coming in, adding new frameworks into their projects, setting up their projects, and getting them to run can be daunting. A dependency manager like Composer for PHP solves this issue. It is considered the "glue between all projects", and there is a good reason for that. Composer uses JSON to keep a track of all the dependencies for a given project. Composer's primary job is to download libraries from remote locations and store them locally. To inform Composer as to what libraries we need, we would need to set up the composer.json file. This file keeps a track of all the specific libraries, their versions, and the environments that a given library should be deployed to. For example, a unit-testing framework library should never make it to production. There was an instance in an old company where a colleague of mine who was randomly testing our production instance deleted the whole user table by running a unit test; we had to recover the whole user table from the previous night's database back ups.

Let's quickly dive in and see how JSON is being used to handle dependency management.

```
composer.json          x
1
2    {
3
4        "require":{
5            "php": ">=5.4.7"
6        },
7        "require-dev":{
8            "phpunit/phpunit": "3.7.*"
9        }
10
11   }
12
```

composer.json

In the `composer.json` file, we are adding two requirements to install a specific version of PHP and PHPUnit. Once the file is added to the project, we can use Composer's `install` command to install these dependencies. Composer also comes with an `update` command that takes care of any updates that are made for a given package.

 For more information about Composer, please visit `http://www.getcomposer.org`.

`Node.js` is a popular software platform that uses the JSON data format for tracking dependencies. **Node Packaged Modules (NPM)** is the package manager that developers use for installing and integrating external modules into their code. For every `Node.js` project, there is a `package.json` file in the document root that keeps track of all the metadata, such as the name of the project, the name of the author, the version number, the required modules to run that project, and the underlying daemons or engines that are required to run the project. Let's take a peek at an example `package.json` file from one of my `Node.js` projects.

```
package.json                    x
1
2   {
3       "name": "TestNodeJSProject",
4       "version": "0.0.1",
5       "author": "Sai Sriparasa <sai.sriparasa@test.com>",
6       "dependencies": {
7           "async": "0.1.18",
8           "connect": "1.8.6",
9           "connect-assetmanager": "0.0.27",
10          "connect-auth": "0.5.1",
11          "connect-mongo": "0.1.7",
12          "cron": "0.3.0",
13          "email": "0.2.5",
14          "emailjs": "0.2.8",
15          "express": "2.5.10",
16          "express-form": "0.6.2",
17          "express-messages": "0.0.2",
18          "eyes": "0.1.7",
19          "fbgraph": "0.2.1",
20          "facebook-sdk": "0.3.2",
21          "jade": "0.26.0",
22          "moment": "1.7.0",
23          "mongodb": "1.0.2",
24      },
25      "engines": {"node": "0.6.x", "npm": "1.0.x"}
26  }
```

package.json

The package.json file is a big JSON object that keeps a track of metadata, such as the project's name, author's details, and the required modules.

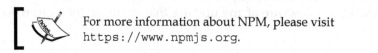

For more information about NPM, please visit https://www.npmjs.org.

JSON for storing metadata

On the same line as dependency managers, JSON is also used to store metadata for software projects. Prior to JSON becoming popular, the configurations and metadata were either stored in a text file or in language-specific files, such as config.php for PHP, config.py for Python, and config.js for JavaScript. All these can now be replaced by a language-independent config.json file; use a JSON library for non-JavaScript libraries to parse it. Let's take a quick look at an example config.json file:

```
config.json              x    schema.json           x
1
2   {
3
4       "PROJECT":"test project",
5       "ENV":"DEV",
6       "AUTOLOAD":[
7                   "class1.php",
8                   "class2.php",
9                   "class3.php"
10          ],
11      "EXCLUDE":[
12                  "project_x",
13                  "vendor"
14          ],
15      "RECURSIVE":"true"
16
17  }
18
```

config.json

In the config.json file, we store the metadata as a JSON object. We are specifying important information such as the project name, the environment of the project (which varies based on the server that the file is located on), any classes that have to be autoloaded during bootstrapping the application, and any classes or folders that we would want to exclude. Finally, using the RECURSIVE key, we also specify that there are folders and those folders have files.

Bootstrapping is the startup process for an application, in which we prepare that application to serve its purpose.

Once we have the config.json file available, we can use the json.loads method in Python or we can use the json_decode method in PHP to parse through the config object to retrieve the data. The JSON objects can also be used to store the database schema; this helps the rest of the development team to update their database schema when one developer on the team makes a change to the database. A smart way to handle this would be by writing a trigger on this schema.json file, and if there is an update to that file, the schema in the database has to be updated to reflect the new changes via the database migration scripts. Let's take a quick look at an example schema.json file.

```json
{

    "client":{
            "id":{
                    "type":"int",
                    "size":11,
                    "primaryKey":"true",
                    "required":"true"
                },
            "name":{
                    "type":"varchar",
                    "size":255,
                    "required":"true"
            },
            "enabled":{
                    "type":"tinyint",
                    "size":4,
                    "required":"true",
                    "defaultValue":1
            }
    }
}
```

schema.json

In the `schema.json` example, we are building the schema JSON object that will store the database schema information. `client` is the name of the table in our schema. The `client` table has three columns — the ID, name, and status of the client, that is, whether the client is enabled or disabled. Each of the columns contains the column JSON object that provides the schema information, such as the datatype and size of the column, whether it has a default value or a primary key constraint.

Comparisons with YAML

YAML is another software language-agnostic data interchange format that is slowly gaining popularity. **YAML is a recursive acronym for YAML Ain't Markup Language**, and is commonly used to store metadata such as configurations, schemas, and properties. YAML is considered a human-readable data serialization standard and depends on white spaces, positioning, and simple characters for line terminators, similar to popular scripting languages such as Ruby and Python. YAML is particular about the spacing between the elements and is not tab friendly. Similar to JSON, YAML key/value pairs are separated by a colon. Similar to text formatting, hyphens are used to indicate list items, unlike JSON where the list items are placed in an array or a child object. Since YAML is software language-agnostic, we would need parsers to understand the contents in that file. Such parsers are available for most of the popular languages such as PHP, Python, C++, Ruby, and JavaScript. Let's build the `config.json` file in YAML to understand what YAML is.

```
PROJECT: "test project"
ENV: "DEV"
AUTOLOAD:
    - "class1.php"
    - "class2.php"
    - "class3.php"
EXCLUDE:
    - "project_x"
    - "vendor"
RECURSIVE: "true"
```

config.yaml

Similar to our config JSON object, the YAML file contains all the data; the difference is in how the data is being arranged — as a list of items — and in how spacing and positioning are used to arrange lists of data. There are multiple YAML resources that are available on the Internet to validate, serialize, and unserialize the YAML data.

 For more information about YAML, please visit `http://www.yaml.org`, which is represented in YAML format.

Summary

JSON is quickly becoming the most popular data interchange format on the Internet, but it is not limited to data exchange. We can also use JSON to store metadata for dependency managers, package managers, configuration managers, and schema data stores. We were introduced to YAML, which is considered as an alternative to JSON. In the next chapter, we will look at the different resources that we can use to debug, validate, and format JSON.

8
Debugging JSON

JSON has grown leaps and bounds in the last few years, due to which there is an abundance of freely available resources to understand the JSON object we are working with. As we have discussed earlier, JSON can be used for multiple purposes, and it is important to understand the simple things that might break JSON, such as ignoring double quotes, or a trailing comma on the last item in the JSON object, or the wrong content-type being sent over by the web server. In this chapter, let us go over the different ways, in which we can debug, validate, and format JSON.

Using the developer tools

Almost all of the top browsers, such as Mozilla Firefox, Google Chrome, Safari, and Internet Explorer, have powerful debugging tools that help us understand the requests that are being made, and the responses that are coming back. JSON could either be part of the request, or be part of the response. Google Chrome, Safari and newer versions of Internet Explorer are shipped out with built-in developer tools. Firebug is a very popular web development toolkit that is available for Mozilla Firefox. Firebug is an external plugin and has to be installed on the browser; it is one of the earliest web development toolkits that was built to assist web developers while using Firefox.

[To install Firebug, please visit http://getfirebug.com/, and click on **Install Firebug** on the landing page.]

These developer tools provide access to the HTML DOM tree, and give us a real-time understanding of how the HTML elements are arranged on the page. The developer tools come with a network (or **Net**) tab that allows us to keep a track of all the resources such as the images, JavaScript files, CSS files, flash media, and any asynchronous calls that the client is making. The console window is another popular feature that is built into the developer tools. As the name suggests, this window provides us a runtime JavaScript console to test any on-the-fly scripts. To fire up the developer tools on Firefox, load the web page into a web browser, and right-click on the web page; this will give us a list of options, choose **Inspect Element with Firebug**. To load the developer tools on Google Chrome and Safari, right-click on a web page and click on **Inspect Element** from the list of the options. When working on Safari, keep in mind that the developer tools have to be enabled; to enable the developer tools, click on the **Safari** menu item, choose **Preferences** and click on the **Advanced** tab, and check **Show develop menu in menu Bar** to view the developer tools. On Internet Explorer, hit the *F12* key on your keyboard to fire up the developer tools window. In *Chapter 4, AJAX Calls with JSON Data*, we made our first asynchronous call to a live web server to request the JSON data using jQuery. Let us use that program and debug the data using developer tools; for this example we will be using the Firefox web browser:

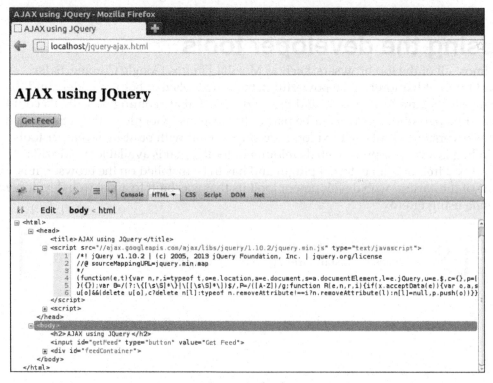

jquery-ajax.html

On page load, when a user right-clicks and chooses the **Inspect Element with Firebug** option, the **HTML** tab is loaded up by default and the user gets to see the HTML DOM. In our example, we had bound a `click` event handler to the **Get Feed** button. Let us look at the console output after the button was clicked; to view the output in the console window, click on the **Console** tab:

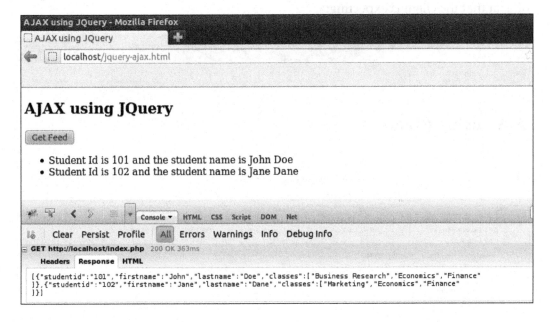

Once the response is retrieved, the JSON feed is logged into the **Response** tab on the console window. It is important to understand the JSON feed in order to parse it, and the developer tools' console window provides us a simple way to analyze the JSON feed. Let us continue our research on the developer tools and visit the **Net** tab in Firefox, to understand how the client and the server communicate the content type of data that the client is expecting:

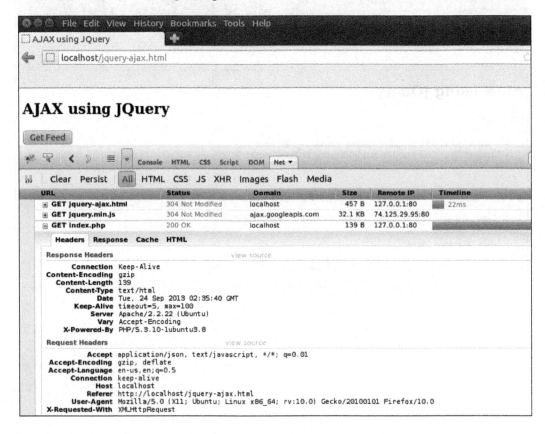

In the Net window, we should begin by clicking on the URL for the asynchronous call, which is being made to index.php. Once that link is clicked, in the **Headers** section we should observe the **Accept** header, which is expecting the application/json **Multipurpose Internet Mail Extensions (MIME)** type, and the **X-Requested-With** header is **XMLHttpRequest**, which notifies that this is an asynchronous request. The **Response** tab in the Net window is the same as the **Response** tab in the console window, and it will display the JSON feed for this request. Throughout this book, we have extensively used the console.log method that prints the data onto the console window, which is another helpful feature of the developer tools.

Validating JSON

Similar to our debugging resources, there are a lot of popular web tools that help us with validating JSON that we build. **JSONLint** is one of the most popular web tools that are available for validating our JSON feeds.

 When we are using a server-side program such as PHP, Python, or Java, the built-in JSON encoding libraries generate the JSON feed, and normally the feed will be a valid JSON feed.

JSONLint has a very straightforward interface that allows the user to paste the JSON they want to validate, and returns either a success message or an error message based on the JSON feed that we paste. Let us begin by validating a bad piece of JSON to see the error message that would be returned, and then let us fix it to view the success message. For this example, I will copy the `students` feed from the previous example, and add a trailing comma at the end of the second element:

```
 1  [
 2    {
 3      "studentid": "101",
 4      "firstname": "John",
 5      "lastname": "Doe",
 6      "classes": [
 7        "Business Research",
 8        "Economics",
 9        "Finance"
10      ]
11    },
12    {
13      "studentid": "102",
14      "firstname": "Jane",
15      "lastname": "Dane",
16      "classes": [
17        "Marketing",
18        "Economics",
19        "Finance"
20      ]
21    },
```

Validate   JSON Lint is an idea from Arc90's Kindling   FAQ
Kindling

Results

```
Parse error on line 21:
        ]    },    ]
------------------^
Expecting 'STRING', 'NUMBER', 'NULL', 'TRUE', 'FALSE', '{', '['
```

Notice that we have added a trailing comma to the last item in our JSON object, and the best part about JSONLint is the descriptive error message. We have encountered a **Parse error**, and to make life simple, the message also gives us the line number where the error could be. The parser is expecting a string, or a number, or a null, or a Boolean value, and because we have supplied none, we are encountering this error. In order to fix this error, we will either have to add a new item to that JSON object to justify the comma, or we will have to get rid of the comma, as there are no items ahead.

As soon as we remove the trailing comma and validate it, we get the success message. Ease of use and descriptive messages have made JSONLint one of the goto websites for JSON validation.

 To work with JSONLint, please visit `http://www.jsonlint.com`.

Formatting JSON

JSONLint is not just an online JSON validator, it also helps us format JSON and makes it look pretty. Often JSON feeds are big in size, and an online editor that provides a tree structure to traverse through the JSON object is always helpful. **JSON Editor Online** is one of my favorite online editors to work with and format the big JSON objects, as it provides an easy to navigate tree structure.

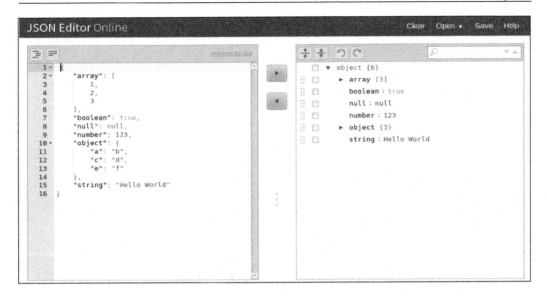

 To work with JSON Editor Online, please visit
http://www.jsoneditoronline.org.

We begin by pasting our JSON example code into the window on the left-hand side,
and click on the right arrow button in the middle to generate our tree structure. Once
we make the changes to the tree structure, we can click on the left arrow button to
format our data, making it ready to use elsewhere.

Summary

Debugging, validating, and formatting are three things that developers can never
ignore. In this chapter, we have looked at resources such as the developer tool kits
for the browsers for debugging, how we can utilize these developer tool kits, and
also saw how to use JSONLint for validation and JSON Editor Online for formatting.

This is the end of *JavaScript and JSON Essentials*, targeted to provide you with an
in-depth insight of how data can be stored and transferred in the JSON data format.
We have had hands-on experience of transferring JSON via HTTP asynchronous
requests within the same domain, and HTTP asynchronous requests across domains.
We have also looked at alternative implementations of how the JSON data format
can be used. This is a solid start to a long journey of understanding JSON to develop
interactive and responsive web applications.

Summary

Index

json.loads() method 28
JSONP
  about 74
  implementation 75-77
jsonp GET parameter 74

L

LAMP 46
LAMP server 47
Linux 46
Linux, Apache, MySQL, and PHP. *See*
    LAMP
looping statements
  using 34

M

MIME 17, 100
multiline comments 8
Multipurpose Internet Mail Extensions. *See*
    MIME
myCallback function 74

N

Node.js 91
Node Packaged Modules (NPM)
  about 91
  URL 92

O

objects
  about 12
  accessing 34
  creating 13
  in JSON, accessing 31-34
onreadystatechange 55
onreadystateChange callback 56
onreadystatechange method 55

P

package.json file 91, 92
PHP
  about 24
  script, running 25

POST AJAX call
  making, with JSON data 62-72
POST request method 62
Python 27, 28

R

readyState property 55
RECURSIVE key 92
Reddit site 73
request object 54
Response tab 100

S

same domain policy 73
same origin policy 73
schema.json file 93
scripting languages 89
semi colon (;) 7
send() method 56
server-side call
  avoiding 72
single line comments 8
sudo 46
sudo tasksel command 46
synchronous request, HTTP request 44

T

tasksel package 46
titleCount variable 38
titles variable 39

U

update command 91

V

variables
  declaring in JavaScript, var keyword used 8
  in JavaScript 7
var keyword
  used, for declaring variables in JavaScript 8

W

web server 43
while_employees_traversal.html file 35
while loop 34, 38

X

XML 15
XMLHttpRequest 55, 100
XMLHTTPRequest API 44
XMLHTTPRequest JavaScript object 44
XMLHttpRequest object 54, 56, 57
XML messages 15
X-Requested-With header 100

Y

YAML Ain't Markup Language (YAML)
about 94
config.json file, building 94
URL 95

Thank you for buying
JavaScript and JSON Essentials

About Packt Publishing

Packt, pronounced 'packed', published its first book "*Mastering phpMyAdmin for Effective MySQL Management*" in April 2004 and subsequently continued to specialize in publishing highly focused books on specific technologies and solutions.

Our books and publications share the experiences of your fellow IT professionals in adapting and customizing today's systems, applications, and frameworks. Our solution based books give you the knowledge and power to customize the software and technologies you're using to get the job done. Packt books are more specific and less general than the IT books you have seen in the past. Our unique business model allows us to bring you more focused information, giving you more of what you need to know, and less of what you don't.

Packt is a modern, yet unique publishing company, which focuses on producing quality, cutting-edge books for communities of developers, administrators, and newbies alike. For more information, please visit our website: www.packtpub.com.

About Packt Open Source

In 2010, Packt launched two new brands, Packt Open Source and Packt Enterprise, in order to continue its focus on specialization. This book is part of the Packt Open Source brand, home to books published on software built around Open Source licences, and offering information to anybody from advanced developers to budding web designers. The Open Source brand also runs Packt's Open Source Royalty Scheme, by which Packt gives a royalty to each Open Source project about whose software a book is sold.

Writing for Packt

We welcome all inquiries from people who are interested in authoring. Book proposals should be sent to author@packtpub.com. If your book idea is still at an early stage and you would like to discuss it first before writing a formal book proposal, contact us; one of our commissioning editors will get in touch with you.

We're not just looking for published authors; if you have strong technical skills but no writing experience, our experienced editors can help you develop a writing career, or simply get some additional reward for your expertise.

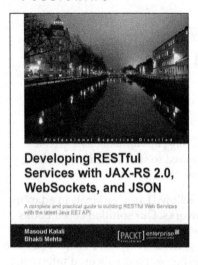

Object-Oriented JavaScript - Second Edition

ISBN: 978-1-84969-312-7   Paperback: 382 pages

Learn everything you need to know about OOJS in this comprehensive guide

1. Think in JavaScript

2. Make object-oriented programming accessible and understandable to web developers

3. Apply design patterns to solve JavaScript coding problems

4. Learn coding patterns that unleash the unique power of the language

Social Data Visualization with HTML5 and JavaScript

ISBN: 978-1-78216-654-2   Paperback: 104 pages

Leverage the power of HTML5 and JavaScript to build compelling visualizations of social data from Twitter, Facebook, and more

1. Learn how to use JavaScript to create compelling visualizations of social data

2. Use the d3 library to create impressive SVGs

3. Master OAuth and how to authenticate with social media sites

Please check **www.PacktPub.com** for information on our titles